D0087386

Quantification in the
History of Political Thought

Recent Titles in
Contributions in Political Science
Series Editor: Bernard K. Johnpoll

Quantification in the History of Political Thought

TOWARD A QUALITATIVE APPROACH

Robert Schware

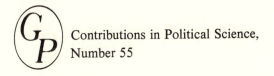

Contributions in Political Science,
Number 55

GREENWOOD PRESS
Westport, Connecticut ● London, England

Library of Congress Cataloging in Publication Data

Schware, Robert, 1952–
  Quantification in the history of political
thought.

  (Contributions in political science; no. 55
ISSN 0147–1066)
  Bibliography: p.
  Includes index.
  1. Political science—History. 2. Political
statistics—History. I. Title. II. Series.
JA81.S347   320'.09   80–1704
ISBN 0–313–22228–2 (lib. bdg.)

Copyright © 1981 by Robert Schware

All rights reserved. No portion of this book may be
reproduced, by any process or technique, without the
express written consent of the publisher.

Library of Congress Catalog Card Number: 80–1704
ISBN: 0–313–22228–2
ISSN: 0147–1066

First published in 1981

Greenwood Press
A division of Congressional Information Service, Inc.
88 Post Road West, Westport, Connecticut 06881

Printed in the United States of America

10 9 8 7 6 5 4 3 2 1

JA
81
S347

To my mother and father,
and the memory of my uncle,
with love and respect.

6/4/82 YP 23.00

486047

To my mind the most striking expression of [the American's moral] materialism is his singular preoccupation with quantity.

George Santayana

Contents

Acknowledgments

I am deeply grateful for the encouragement and support I have received to complete this work from the London School of Economics and Political Science Graduate School. I owe also a debt of gratitude to Robert Orr for his helpful suggestions and comments.

Quantification in the
History of Political Thought

Introduction

> Let us calculate.
> — *Leibnitz*
>
> To know mathematics not politics.
> — *Hobbes*

This work examines an idea that has central, albeit neglected, importance to the Western orientation of thought: quantification. Indeed it has become so familiar to modern thought that it is a commonplace. We speak, for instance, of the "quantum revolution," the "quantitative base of democracy," the "quantitative rather than qualitative standards erected by judicial bodies," and "the quantitative measure showing we're winning this war." In political science, to take one example, the tools of learning conform to and even attempt to elicit the present advances in technology; scales of measurement, control groups, public opinion polls, game theories, chi-square tests, and other devices are in vogue. Central to the whole field is the use of numerical tests and quantified procedures.

Quantitative formulations have permeated political discovery as a whole. At the end of the nineteenth century, for instance, Lord Kelvin remarked, "When you can measure what you are speaking about and express it in numbers, you know something about it; and when you cannot measure it, when you cannot express it in numbers, your knowledge is of a meagre and unsatisfactory kind."[1] (Part of this comment has become immortal by its inscription on the University of Chicago's Social Science Research Building.) Not long afterward, Arthur Bentley, a collaborator of John Dewey, expressed in more certain terms the belief that "it is impossible to attain scientific treatment of material that will not submit itself to measurement in some form. Measure conquers chaos."[2] William Munro's 1908 presidential address to the American Political Science Association throws some further light on this tendency toward the quantitative description of political phenomena:

> Political science should borrow by analogy from the new physics a determination to get rid of intellectual insincerities concerning the nature of sovereignty, the general will, natural rights, and the freedom of the individual, the consent of the governed, majority rule. . . . In place of these formulas it should seek to find concepts that will stand the test of actual operations and upon these it should begin to rebuild itself by an intimate observation of the actualities.[3]

And, more recently Paul Lazarsfeld has voiced a similar attitude: "The very complexity of social events requires a language of quantity."[4] Numerous other examples could be provided to show the great, if not overwhelming, emphasis put on quantitative discourse.

It becomes necessary to remind ourselves that the intellectual equipment of politics in the past had a character quite different from the purely empirical and mathematical conceptions of modern politics. Indeed the literature, from Plato to Hegel, is filled with expressions of contempt and hostility toward quantitative knowledge as such. Gradually and progressively, however, the notion of quantity has become increasingly important and springs up more and more frequently. The emphasis of this essay is, to be sure, less contemporary than historical. I have tried to assess carefully not merely the term *quantification* but the assemblage of related terms that embrace it, such as *quantity, quantifiable, quantum, quality,* and *qualitative.* This, of course, has meant more than simply compiling a list of the various uses of the term.

I have attempted here to provide a conceptual framework of the term as invoked by political theorists. Further, I have tried to indicate in a distinctive way the roots and pedigree of quantitative thinking— that is, the introduction of counting, well-defined rules, and measurable uniformities into the judgments we make about politics. As such, this book investigates different contextual uses of quantification with reference to specific theorists and in terms of political problems. Such an account cannot ignore the term's philosophical and scientific significance, both of which have helped to determine the nature and content of quantification and are thus bound up with it.

The primary aim of chapter 1 is to give a perspective on the principal interpretations of the terms *quantity* and *quality*. It does not pretend to come anywhere close to being exhaustive, nor is the selection entirely random. I have chosen those contributions from the spectrum of political philosophers who seem to have had a distinctive, if not pre-eminent, role in the development of views about the subject matter. Under the limits of space, equally important *oeuvres* must be excluded, such as Leibnitz's explanation of quantity and quality as possessing universal characteristics, and Russell and Whitehead's regard for these concepts as reducible to purely logical assumptions. The importance of these, among other notable contributions, to the discussion of quantification is worth careful study.

I have set aside purely chronological lines of development at first. Instead I have endeavored to place the range of thinkers on this matter into a wide, coherent, and systematic context. As a starting point, an operative distinction may be made, I suggest, between those theorists who employ the terms unrelated to each other by way of distinction and others who use them by way of opposition. The former way of conceiving these concepts considers them as distinct moments, independent, and unresolved into any particular unity. Common to those theorists who treat quantity and quality in a distinct fashion is the view that these notions are serviceable in terms of their own political philosophies. They share the feature of considering the terms with a view to applying them in various uses. The terms function in these analyses as data for generalization that seem grounded upon an impulse toward power of some sort. Accordingly Bacon's *Novum Organum* constructs not theories about quantity but, with the aid of the natural sciences and mathematics, advocates the harnessing of nature from facts already collected about energy, force, acceleration, heat, and so on. Petty's *The Political Arithmetick* assesses the strength of England vis-à-vis France in terms of statistical and demographic criteria. Locke's *An Essay Concerning Human Understanding* describes primary and secondary qualities; the former are purely quantitative in character, whereas the latter are essentially powers or properties that cause ideas in our minds. Bentham's felicific calculus expresses the mathematical spirit of English utilitarianism; his *Principles of Morals and Legislation* is an attempt to establish fixed standards of punishment designed to curtail the misuse of human powers by criminals.

And in *Capital* Marx takes the analogy of the transition from quantity to quality from the realm of natural science and applies it to the breakdown of capitalist production and the consequent transition to socialist society.

The other way of conceiving quantity and quality in the history of political thought is through those theorists who speak of the terms not as standards or prescriptions but as antinomial propositions or assertions and hence by way of opposition. In these cases the terms are expounded as two moments of a single determination. Political philosophers who fit this situation have not attempted to utilize the terms in any specific way but only to conceive them. They have made the terms into objects of cognition that are coherent and related to experience only in their initial form. Here the conceptual terms become merely tools for us to gain knowledge or lay the basic assumptions about phenomena in general. The point of these investigations is to establish the truth of the terms as forms of consciousness without reference to any particular material sphere of existence. In this sense, although Plato, Aristotle, Kant, and Hegel, for instance, each provides his own distinctive account of the terms under investigation, the philosophers can nevertheless be considered at one with each other in operating within an oppositional framework.

Unquestionably it is not enough to plot the various conceptions of quantity and quality over time or to place them merely in the broad distinctive-oppositional framework as suggested here. The tendency of political thought after Aristotle has been an accentuation of quantity over quality. Confessedly, however, Cartesian rationalism is a far cry from Bentham's introduction of a hedonic calculus into government. To be sure, the conceptual treatment and application of the notion of quantification is not static. Rather it must be seen in all its dynamic aspects, movement, and successive relations. These have taken different forms in various political, philosophical, and scientific contexts. It is therefore necessary to consider in greater detail in what capacity and in what ways quantity and quantitative features have been emphasized. In order to help fill the gap in research on this matter, the following chapters will assess the importance of quantity and measurement in the writings of Bacon, Hobbes, and Mill. I thereby hope to draw attention to this much neglected field of inquiry (in the historical sense) and, in the process, provide an adequate knowledge of it in three very worthwhile political writers who may be generally recognized as instrumental to any discussion of this subject.

It does not seem to me that the relation among these particular theorists is as important to study as the context and dependence upon certain quantitative characteristics. That such an analysis is valuable depends on a tacit acceptance of the limited nature of this investigation, for it does not profess to examine these theoretical programs in toto; rather it seeks to shed some light on the nature of a particular subject matter of the systems themselves.

In presenting an account of the important approaches to the study of quantity and quality I have tried to abstain from passing any sort of judgment on the particular mode of inquiry and on the various considerations of the subject that have appeared in the inquiry itself. Doubtless this is not the only way the import and nature of quantification can be disclosed. The conclusion is perhaps less impartial. Having analyzed certain positivistic principles bequeathed to posterity by a few of the major writers of political thought, the general problem is thus to attempt to overcome these one-dimensional, ready-made conceptions. My aim here is to examine the lines along which we may make qualitative appraisals of the notions of politics. Certainly much still needs to be done in the form of ongoing critical evaluations that will show the limited and distorted nature of quantitative conceptions and mere numerical approaches so characteristic of our age. Although the eradication of this flight to formula making is more than a pipedream, it nevertheless still has a long trajectory.

Notes

1. Lord Kelvin, *Popular Lectures and Address* (London, 1889), vol. 1, p. 73. Kelvin's remark is strikingly similar to Condorcet's comment in his *Sketch for a Historical Picture of the Progress of the Human Mind*, trans. J. Barraclough (London, 1955), p. 190: "If this evidence cannot be weighted and measured, and if these effects cannot be subjected to precise measurement, then we cannot know exactly how much good or evil they contain."

2. Arthur Fisher Bentley, *The Process of Government* (New York, 1908), p. 200.

3. William B. Munro, "Physics and Politics—An Old Analogy Revised," *American Political Science Review* 22 (February 1928): 10. See also "Reports on the National Conference on the Science of Politics," *American*

Political Science Review 18 (February 1924) and 19 (February 1925).

4. Paul F. Lazarsfeld, in the introduction to Han Zeisel's *Say It with Figures* (New York, 1947), p. xi. For readers interested in more than a historical point of view, see the excellent bibliographical article on quantitative investigations in the field of political science by Richard Fagen: "Some Contributions of Mathematical Reasoning to the Study of Politics," *American Political Science Review* 55 (December 1976): 888–99.

Perspectives on Quantity and Quality (1)

> . . . all qualities have a
> quantity . . .
> — *Freud*

The distinction between quantity and quality as explanatory concepts, or quantitative and qualitative types of analyses, has generally had a strong connection to the field of chemistry. Qualitative analyses—those that seek to identify the *qualis* or kinds of constituent elements of organic or inorganic matter—are distinguished from quantitative analyses, which involve a determination of the *quantus* (how much) of elements that a single substance or mixture contains. Only by first identifying an element in terms of what it is or what it contains can a chemist proceed to weigh or estimate its value and then organize other elements into a particular system of measurements.

Although quantitative and qualitative approaches to understanding reality have been classed customarily within the exact sciences, this is bypassed almost everywhere. Today the basic components of such investigations have been assimilated and re-situated in the so-called modern social sciences, including history, economics, politics, and psychology. Indeed in the course of time, quantitative reasoning has eclipsed qualitative reasoning. The change, reaching back long before the Enlightenment and certainly most conceivably (though not culminating) with the rise of positivism, is nevertheless exceedingly difficult to localize. The swing did not emerge like a tidal wave, yet it can be viewed as something more than a mere intimation. It is perhaps useful to begin with the seventeenth century as a point of departure, although it is a misleading oversimplification to suggest that this is when quantitative thinking first came to dominate the rational sciences.

To some scholars, the uncertainty of where first to encounter the ideal of exact, scientific political knowledge is totally incomprehensible; precise, calculated, and well-measured knowledge in the domain of politics was wanting until Machiavelli. In the sense that he introduced new methods, based on pragmatic experience and historical extractions, which established definite principles or rules governing the behavior of men, he may justly be the founder of modern political philosophy. But Machiavelli did not think and work in the spirit of science; rather he relied strictly on the past and offered his secular advice on the state as a "work of art." "The conduct of Rome must be imitated in every particular," he declared in *The Prince*. However, what distinguishes sixteenth-century Florence from seventeenth-century England is the preoccupation with laws of nature as opposed to Machiavelli's deductions based on examples from history. Thinking of this kind, in terms of abstract bodies free of historical precedents but inextricably guided by degrees of motion, did not emerge until Galileo's investigations. Coexistent with Galileo's discoveries into the laws of nature, the laws of civil society were identified as fundamental presuppositions of human behavior, replacing classical, ethical standpoints.

The dominant characteristic of the late sixteenth century and the pre-Newtonian period of the seventeenth century was its predilection for measurement. This resulted from the close interconnection and overlap between the experimental sciences and mathematics. The focal point in interpreting the true reality of nature, according to Galileo, was mathematics. He conceived the universe as a "mathematical manifold," which assured us in expressly formulated truths that nature could be known unsupported by evidence from our senses. Galileo recognized that whatever little we learned through mathematical science was beyond doubt. Galilean science thus revealed that the flux and purpose of natural reality could be conceived and defined with progressive exactness. Hence all chance is unconditionally excluded, and accurate, indifferent rules of reason thus arrived at.

What is especially significant for the seventeenth century as a point of departure is that the accurate forms of knowledge traditionally applied to measure, number, and weight now became the object of political thought. Nowhere is this more evident than in Hobbes's introductory statement to his *Elements of Philosophy*:

I confess that that part of philosophy by which magnitude and figures are computed, is highly improved. But because I have not observed the like advancement in the other parts of it, my purpose is, as far forth as I am able, to lay open the few and first Elements of Philosophy in general, as so many seeds from which pure and true Philosophy may hereafter spring up by little and little.[1]

Hobbes, among others, attempted to extend the media of mechanics and mathematics into civil philosophy.[2] *Mad mathesis*, as Pope referred to it, became a point of leverage for making the seemingly inaccurate and indefinite neoclassical orientation satisfactorily certain, if not objective. Whether the principles of political philosophy can be grounded as such is a moot point at this stage. What is significant, however, is that social and philosophical investigation became infected with mechanics and mathematics, viewed, as they were, as sciences par excellence. By highlighting quantity and thinking primarily in terms of counting and calculation, quality and qualitative understanding became blurred and were relegated to a background status.

An understanding of the intellectual origins and development of these notions perhaps is approached best from a conceptual level by elaborating the character of the terms as used by political theorists in the past. Their inner relations, along with the ways in which they have been tailored to fit the content of the political problem at hand, will be the chief concerns of this enterprise. We now turn to the detail of the concepts themselves.

The Tradition of Opposition

Although it is not unusual today to view quantity and quality as a pair of opposites, this expressive dualism had not been realized before Plato's time. This mode of presentation, whereby the terms are treated as intrinsically bound up with one another, is a product of Plato's dialectical thinking.[3] Everything that admits of generation, says Plato in the *Phaedo*, issues from their opposites. This includes objects of every sort, actions, and ideas. In this way Plato deduces beauty from ugliness, right from wrong, one from many, and so on.

Hence wherever there is becoming or movement, there is oscillation between opposites. The immediate question that arises is which comes first: quality or quantity, light and dark, and so forth? But according to Plato, this is a misleading question in that it presupposes the exclusive existence of both categories. Dialectical understanding, on the contrary, seeks to show that any one category, taken on its own, is partial and abstract without its vital opposite. But what specifically does Plato say about quality and quantity?

In the *Theaetetus*, Plato brings the notion of quality into the foreground and attempts a definition that is alien to the dialectical process. As Socrates tells Theodorus in the dialogue, "Perhaps this word 'quality' strikes you as queer and uncouth and you don't understand it as a general expression."[4] Subsequently Plato distinguishes between a quality and what we may call a qualifier. Hotness and whiteness, according to Plato, are not properties of a thing itself. These qualifiers merely serve to denote a particular type of change that occurs in a thing or agent. Hence they are accidental in nature in the sense that they are potentially common to several or many things instead of one thing. For Plato, a quality is a constituent element of a thing; that is, it is an essential feature of a given entity rather than a contingent property. It follows that a quality is a form or universal that merely means that it is more than this particular attribute (perhaps brown) or that particular attribute (perhaps shape). Qualities, then, are not attributes or properties as such; still, for Plato, qualities do not exist exclusive from these qualifiers.

This also applies to the quantity of a certain body. Thus, in the latter dialogue, *Philebus*, Socrates asks how qualifying terms such as *hotter, lower,* and *slightly* admit of anything else but an absolute unlimited.[5] That is, their character is purely of a "more or less" and hence incompatible with "definite quantity."

Plato says nothing of the mutual interaction and dialectical reconstitution of quantity and quality, but his main thought is quite clear. It is that quantity and quality are an antimonious combination whose character cannot be reduced to sensible aids or affectations. They are, as the *Republic* tells us, "pure ideas moving on through ideas to ideas and ending with ideas."[6]

On closer examination, however, Plato's rather Heraclitean view of motion and experience as an endless stream of flux and reflux bespeaks a great deal about the character of quantities and qualities. According to Plato in the *Theaetetus*, there are two kinds of change: locomotion and alteration.[7] The former involves the emission of energy without a change of place, whereas alteration involves a change of orbit (or leap) from one spectrum to another. In the latter motion, neither a thing's quality nor its quantity remains stable. In the movement from youth to old age, for instance, both the person's qualitative position and quanta, or years, undergo decisive change. Both are definite changes, yet in themselves they are fluid.

Plato's pupil Aristotle provided a distinctive delimitation of the terms quite different from the dialectical edifice built by his mentor. He focused not on the contradiction between the terms but on the determinations arising from the relations between them. His analysis develops the inherent relations of these coordinates in terms of logical and political categories. Aristotle suggests that any categorical classification of the properties of man, as such, must begin with the questions "What is man?" or "What is the substance of a thing?" The information derived from such investigations can be classified according to substance, quantity, quality, relation, place, time, state, position, action, and passion. These represent the ground of his *Categories*.

At the outset, the order in which Aristotle's categories occurs raises some important questions, for if he does not consider quantity and quality as opposites yet inherently in union with one another, he must envisage one as prior to or prefiguring the other. Unfortunately Aristotle does not give any justification for the ordering of his key categories. To be sure, the same grouping occurs in an earlier work of his, the *Topics*. Although he does not provide us with any reason for classifying quantity before quality, he is not alone in interpreting the nature of reality as primarily quantitative and then possessing quality. Lucretius, Plotinus, Aquinas, Hobbes, Locke, and Boyle, among others, treated nature and experience in a like manner. Aquinas, for example, in his *Summa Theologica* maintained that "quantity is the proximate subject of the qualities that cause alteration." He also wrote, "Quantity is in substance before other sensible qualities are."[8] For Plotinus it was the medium by which reality could be understood: "The Intellectual Cosmos thus a manifold, Number and Quantity arise."[9] And when speaking of primary qualities, both Locke and

Boyle had in mind a thing's original features: solidity, number, motion or rest, and extension.[10]

According to Aristotle, quantity ultimately rests on three principles. First, a quantity cannot have a contrary, another quantity that denies its existence. Thus the first prerequisite of understanding kinds of quantity is knowing whether self-contradiction is an impossibility. For example, a given surface four meters in length constitutes a quantity because it admits of no contrary. Second, a quantity does not yield to a "more or less" kind of judgment; it is a simple substance that possesses a certain and definite amount. This does not deny the fact that one may speak of it in terms of degrees, but these degrees must be positively fixed, certain ones. What we commonly view within the realm of more or less Aristotle refers to as a relative expression. Thus considered, a mountain, for example, is more than something else, say a stone. Third, only a quantity can be considered as equal or unequal, for, as Aristotle remarks, the very nature of non-quantitative things is that their state of existence can be envisaged only in relative terms; they may be similar or dissimilar but never correlatively equal. These are indispensable distinctions.

When Aristotle speaks of qualities, he understands four different subclasses. The first species of qualities that Aristotle recognizes are human states or conditions. He means here accidental virtues, such as health, beauty, and generosity. The second kind of quality is not derived from any condition because it represents a natural or inborn capacity or incapacity. These natural particularities of individuals, such as being crippled, appear distinctively in Plato's theory of qualities as mere properties. In a similar vein, Aristotle's third kind of quality, which he refers to as "affectations," can easily be interpreted as Platonic accidents or qualifiers. If this is true, then Aristotle's conditional qualities can hardly be distinguished from affective qualities. This apparent blur is never satisfactorily cleared up.[11] Turning away from subjective types of qualities, Aristotle presents the final sphere of qualities. Here quality denotes an external representation, such as the straightness of a geometrical shape or the spatio-temporal form of a physical object.

Aristotle's distinction between quantity and quality is not confined to the thicket of categorical demarcations. He also uses the criteria in drawing up what he considers the most desirable sorts of constitutions. However, it cannot be inferred from his designation of quantity and quality in the *Politics* that he considers the terms as fixed and un-mediated, as later political theorists have done. To be sure, it is in the *Politics* that Aristotle illustrates the intimate connection between quantity and quality and the need to invoke these terms as relative to politics and not as blanket terms. Aristotle uses the terminology with respect to ascertaining "what and what sort of constitution is suited to what and what sort of persons."[12]

In the *Politics* Aristotle argues that governments may be classified by reference to the vesting of authority or sovereignty. From the standpoint of who holds political power, Aristotle divided govern-ments according to the One, the Many, and the Few. Thus consid-ered, the basic components of Aristotle's classification are founded on a quantitative trichotomy. But Aristotle has something more in mind than a mere breakdown of political systems. His main concern is to reconcile extremes, which, in turn, would guarantee a fair and smoothly functioning government. First and foremost, Aristotle holds that "quantity and quality must thus be placed in the balance against one another."[13] The distinction between these two claims is quite clear to Aristotle:

By "quality" we mean free birth, wealth, culture, and nobility of descent; by "quantity" we mean superiority in numbers. Now quality may belong to one of the parts which compose a state, and quantity to another. For example, those who are low-born may be more numerous than the high-born, or the poor than the rich; but the superiority in quantity on the one side may not be sufficient to balance the superiority of quality on the other.[14]

The result of this account of quantity and quality was far from for-tuitous. Aristotle shows that societies can be predicated upon pre-cisely these criteria. He elaborates the link between quantity and quality and forms of government in the following way. First, these terms pertain to all kinds of governments and are the main criteria for distinguishing one type of government from another. Where quantity of numbers outweighs the *aristoi* (meaning "the best" or "outstanding excellence" and which Aristotle has in view when he speaks of quality), the most suitable kind of government will be democratic. This is not to say that all democracies are of the same type. Aristotle tells us they will differ depending on whether they are comprised predominantly of farmers, peasants, or mechanics (or industrial workers). We can decide whether a given society is most suitably of the second variety, aristocratic-oligarchic, by an inverse ratio. If the quality of a select few persons outweighs their insignificance in point of quantity, the government will be treated as oligarchic. Finally, if both of these extremes are blunted by an overwhelming middle class, then it is beyond question that a polity will be the most reasonable form of government. According to Aristotle, a polity has important characteristics that democracies and aristocracies lack. Both democracies and aristocracies clearly represent the overstrong extremes of quantity and quality, whereas the polity illustrates the genuine unity of these unmediated excesses. Hence a polity can be regarded as a mean, a measure, or a true sufficiency.

Similarly, Aristotle uses the notions of quality and quantity explicitly with respect to ethics or so-called moral virtues. Virtues, according to Aristotle in the *Ethics*, are divisible in terms of a more or less, excess and defect. Hence every quality (in this sense a disposition toward something, say, honor, pride, wealth, friendship) conforms to certain limits that mold its existence and through which it becomes truly realized. Aristotle defines virtue as "a sort of mean, since it aims at the intermediate," or, as he says elsewhere, "the quantitative equality."[15] Thus, for instance, the mean of wealth is liberality; its excess is fanciful prodigality; and its defect, or formal lower limit, is stinginess or meanness. The mean is the heart of any particular virtue, beyond which there are only inequality and incommensurability.

This view of virtue as containing qualitative and quantitative attributes culminated in Aquinas's theory of divinity as subsisting independent of matter and form. Aquinas held that quantity is essentially twofold: "There is quantity of *bulk* or dimensive quantity, which is to be found only in corporeal things, and has, therefore, no place in God. There is also quantity of *virtue*, which is measured according to the perfection of some nature or form."[16] Here we have a totally different situation from the way in which Aristotle envisaged virtue and quantity. What Aquinas is really talking about is the distinction between corporeal and nonsensible quantity, or what amounts to much the same thing, the differences between physical and mathematical quantity. Built into his meaning of virtue is the belief that quantity need not be present or in fact actually exist. It follows for Aquinas that once we accept that quantities do not exist as realities and that they have a purely logical existence, we can then go on to demonstrate the existence of God without necessarily alluding to matter or dimensive quantity. God and the angels, he asserts in the *Summa Theologica*, find no place in things determined according to bulk or magnitude, "for theirs is a virtual quantity" alone.[17]

Perhaps the most formidable attack on Aristotle's formulations (as opposed to Aquinas's mere extrapolation and re-presentation of the peripatetic doctrines) emerged when Kant set aside the Aristotelian superstructure and proposed in its stead a new foundation of categories. Indeed Kant's transcendental principles afford the clearest point of departure from earlier conceptions of quantity and quality.

Kant began by criticizing Aristotle's catalog as "haphazard" and "unsystematic." Kant's enumeration of twelve categories or "logical functions," as he called them, was not aimed at setting forth "a complete system, but merely the principles of one."[18] For Kant, however, Aristotle had reasoned incorrectly in a far more significant way than merely listing his categories in a "rhapsodic" and arbitrary manner. As Kant notes, the whole idea of basing the categories on expressions "without combination" was misleading; instead Aristotle should have started with judgments. As Kant points out in the *Critique of Pure Reason*, "We can reduce all acts of the understanding to judgments, so that *understanding* may be represented as the *faculty of judging*."[19] We can understand Kant's statement in this way: the mind synthesizes all sensory perceptions under concepts. In other words, we know or are acquainted with an object by relating it to a notion that applies to it. For instance, a sensible object, say a stone, presupposes a corresponding conception of it given in the consciousness.

According to Kant, all of the possible logical functions of judgment are subsumed under a priori categories, for we understand things by means of conceptions that are immediately connected to the categories themselves. It is important to remember that without these categories understanding experience would be futile. In short, because in Kant's theoretical framework phenomena or appearances conform to the categories, it may be said to differ radically from Aristotle's, whose categories classified things or objects.

In turning to Kant's understanding of quantity and quality, it is helpful to make a few preliminary remarks. To begin, the use to which

Kant puts the terms does not have an immediate affinity with the oppositional types of analyses recorded above. That is, Kant does not consider quantity and quality as polar terms or as combinations that necessarily form a unified determination. Kant resists this particular impulse but only insofar as the outer structure of his theory is concerned, for, as we shall see, the dialectical approach is far from inconsequential to the inner elements of his categories.

Second, with regard to the spheres of categories and of judgments, Kant asserts that, without exception, these are limited to twelve: judgments of quantity are universal, particular, or singular; judgments of quality are affirmative, negative, or limited; judgments of relation are categorical, hypothetical, or disjunctive; and judgments of modality are problematical, assertorical, or apodictical. Similarly, Kant's treatment of the categories parallels the triadic development and the logical forms of the judgments themselves. It follows that the dimensions of judgments of quantity (universal, particular, or singular) correspond to the elements of the category of quantity, which comprises unity, plurality, and totality. The same is true of the judgments we make under quality (affirmative, negative, or limited), and the category of quality which embraces reality, negation, and limitation. To judgments of relation correspond the specific forms found in the category of relation: substance and accidents, cause and effect, and intermingling between agent and patient. Last, the three forms of judgments of modality are placed by Kant in connection to the classes within the category of modality, which include possibility and impossibility, existence and nonexistence, and necessity and contingence. Kant provides us with a rather large, albeit limited, horizon. One criticism of him springs to mind at this stage. It consists in the fact that he believed these twelve factors of our recognition exhausted all potential representations. This was a rather naive suggestion and became the central point around which Hegel focused his *Science of Logic*.

For Kant, understanding empirical data is based upon perceptual judgments derived from the knower. Every judgment, so conceived, is the application of one of the categories and coordinates with one of the specific principles that belong to it. This means that every presentation to the understanding embodies two features: perceiving and judging. Thus "all men are rational," for example, falls under the concept of unity under the category quantity and involves a universal judgment at the same time. In the same manner, to say that "Socrates was not rational" involves a negative distinction under the category quality and, correspondingly, a negative judgment. Yet this application of elementary categories and axioms of judgment tells us nothing of the dynamics of the triads themselves.

"It is to be added," says Kant in the transcendental part of his logic, "that the third category in each triad always arises from the combination of the second with the first. Thus Totality is nothing else but Plurality contemplated as Unity; Limitation is merely Reality conjoined with Negation."[20] According to Kant, every category is a concrete embodiment of three phases. The logical structure of quantity, again, is represented by three parts: unity, plurality, and totality. Each of these moments has a peculiar character of its own, which means that they are not subordinated to one another. Rather the positing of one reciprocally determines the others in the sense that they are immediately excluded from the particular act of understanding. Something akin to this exclusion occurs whenever one part of the conception is employed, and the others temporarily disappear.

Thus far we know that the categories are linked to perception in the sense that they refer to objects given in the sensuous world. Equally important is the idea that if these perceptions are to be understood, they must refer to judgments. We also know that the third stage of the triad is generated out of the former two and that by positioning any particular moment, we in turn cancel all of the others. Kant, however, does not stop here, for we still do not have any rule or condition that indicates to which category a given phenomenon applies. Hence we are in need of specific schemata, as Kant calls them, or referential rules to determine the conditions under which objects of experience are subsumed under fundamental concepts and categories.

Kant shows that the schemata, "or the sensuous conception of an object in harmony with the category," can be divided according to each of the categories of understanding.[21] The underlying schema of the category of quantity is number. An object of perception may be considered a quantity only if "it can be cogitated how many times one is placed in it."[22] By this Kant implies that in order to conceive of a thing in terms of quantity, a standard by which to compare objects is required. Weight, for instance, cannot be conceived without constructing a scale whereby objects can be matched in terms of their quantity. In Kant's view, phenomena "cannot be apprehended, that is, received into empirical consciousness otherwise than through the synthesis of a manifold, through which the representations of a determinate space or time are generated; that is to say . . . all phenomena are quantities, and extensive quantities."[23]

The basic schema of the category of quality is degree. Insofar as a sensation generates an intensity, either more or less, it has a definite reference to perception. Whatever its determinate degree, ipso facto it is connected to reality (a subclass of the category of quality), whereas if it is not intense enough to be represented to us, it is accounted under the moment of negation. Such a descension—from a quantum of intensity to a zero intenseness—Kant refers to as a transition from reality to negation. These momenta, or forms of each category, are thus not fixed principles.

I will not sketch the ways in which Kant's remaining categories are schematized or discuss some of the persisting problems in his analysis of knowledge. It is important to note, however, that one of the first things we notice in Kant's writings on politics, history, and morality is that he made no effectual attempt to apply logically the categories of understanding to these spheres. The categories are the means by which we do our thinking; Kant's account of them remains strictly an epistemology. As we shall see, Hegel's work was the first attempt to deduce the categories of knowledge from one another and then to give an account of them through the working out of Spirit, or *Geist*, involving nature, ethics, history, art, and religion. Here we can only note a few instances in Kant's moral philosophy where he is especially concerned with quantitative thinking, particularly in his rejection of the utilitarian formulation of happiness as an essentially quantitative determination.

Kant says in his *Idea for a Universal History* that "human actions, like every other natural event, are determined by universal laws."[24] It is this attitude that is reflected in his methodological conception of the natural and the moral sciences. Everything that happens, in physics as well as in ethics, happens not according to subjective invention but because of either a law of physical nature or a law of human freedom.

It follows from this that if moral laws are valid, they "must hold for all rational beings without distinction."[25] Moral laws, in other words, cannot be conditional on circumstances or particular maxims. Feelings, inclinations, private institutions, and empirical standards could never yield a universal moral code because their content was a product of the subjective purposes and affairs of individuals. What is universal is guided by universal rules. As Kant put it, "Moral principles must be *a priori* and self-validating, rather than dependent upon the particularities of human experience."[26]

What is epoch making in Kant's analysis is the acumen with which he penetrates the pleasure motive of utilitarian ethics and brings to light its shallow content and meaning. The defect of the greatest happiness principle is apparent in the utilitarian manner of representing history. For Kant, history is not governed by the endless pursuit of quantitative increases in happiness:

The quantity of good mixed in man with the evil cannot exceed a certain measure beyond which it would be able to work its way up and thus ever proceed toward the better. Eudaemonism, with its sanguine hopes, therefore, appears to be untenable and to promise little in a prophetic history of humanity in favor of progress endlessly broadening its course toward the good.[27]

Indeed, as Kant argued earlier, "a comparison of the degree of happiness and an advantage of one human class or one generation over another is not even possible."[28]

Brendon Liddell, in his analysis of Kant's *Foundation for a Metaphysics of Morals*, quite rightly points out that Kant's criticism of the greatest happiness principle as an invalid foundation for genuine moral law does not make him an "anti-hedonist."[29]

In Kant's view, the demands of morality are such that our subjective propensities for ever-increasing happiness may have to be ignored completely. Kant makes this clear in *Perpetual Peace*:

Political maxims must not be derived from the welfare or happiness which a single state expects from obedience to them, and thus not from the end which one of them proposes for itself. That is, they must not be deduced from volition as the supreme yet empirical principle of political wisdom, but rather from the pure concept of the duty of right, from the ought whose principle is given *a priori* by pure reason, regardless of what the physical consequences may be.[30]

Elsewhere in response to the rhetorically posed question, "What profit will progress toward the better yield humanity?" Kant prophetically answers, "Not an ever-growing quantity of morality with regard to intention, but an increase of the products of legality in dutiful actions whatever their motives."[31]

If for Kant's political theory the whole structure of moral law must rest on universal truths, the true locus of this standard is in mathematics. A note in *Perpetual Peace* may help to clarify this essential insight into the ultimate standards Kant set for moral actions. As Kant put it, "The possibility of a formula similar to those of mathematics is the only legitimate criterion of a consistent legislation, and without it the so-called *ius certum* must always remain a pious wish. Otherwise we shall have merely general laws (which apply to a great number of cases) as the concept of a law seems to require."[32] Kant sees this very clearly, which is why he repudiates any attempt to ground a moral system and man's freedom on particular, especially quantitative, principles.

In both the sort of classificatory thinking and in the reciprocity of the forms of understanding, Hegel may be said to resemble Kant's critical way of thinking. Not content, however, with Kant's view of the categories as concerned purely with subjective appearances, Hegel endeavored to prove logically that the thing-in-itself could be known through the coexistence of these polar forms. That is, an object may be comprehended as bound up with antinomies that ultimately yield to a unified reality. Hegel begins his *Science of Logic* with an explanation of the nature of this reality. His starting point is how the ordinary consciousness conceives things as being.

The basis of being for Hegel is quality: "Quality is, in the first place the character identical with being; so identical that a thing ceases to be what it is, if it loses its quality."[33] And, in the preface of *The Phenomenology of Mind*, he states again, "When I say Quality, I state simple determinateness; by means of its quality one existence is distinguished from another."[34] In his consideration of being, Hegel confronts one facet of Plato's analysis of quality that is manifest in the above phrase: that a quality is not something that exists by itself. We may suppose that a being is antecedent to experience, a unique peculiarity, indefinitely expandable into its own being-in-itself, but this is to construe abstractly the nature of quality, which invariably refers to its otherness, or as Hegel calls it, its "being-for-others." What he implies is that a quality is determined in contrast with other qualitatively determined beings. Quality is, to be sure, identical with the whole being of a thing. Yellowness or redness, for instance, although contrary aspects of a thing, nevertheless are not identical to its whole character. Thus for Hegel color, and most of what are normally taken for qualities, is an external property a thing owns but, unlike quality, it is not the thing (that is, it is not identical to an object's very being or essence).

The character of being is further delimited by Hegel into finitude and variability. He stresses that being, consisting of real and opposed determinations along with finitude and alterability, consists of moments of physical nature as posited and reflected upon by us. These moments also have being in themselves, independently of the knowing subject and are not merely subjective rational constructs. Nonetheless, in saying that a given quality is finite, Hegel means that its demise is inherent in its own character and that it cannot possibly avoid annulment (for example, life is a movement toward death). This fosters, says Hegel, an immense despair in man's sensibility. Finitude, to be sure, "is the most stubborn category of the understanding . . . because it is qualitative negation pushed to its extreme, and in the singleness of such determination there is no longer left to things an affirmative being distinct from their destiny to perish."[35] This is not to suggest that all immanent determination is negative or finite, for all determinate being has an aspect of positive being and of infinity. Finitude, however, suggests something more than an immanent negative determination. It implies that a frontier or limit becomes prominent and qualitatively distinct. Qualities, therefore, are bound to be replaced by new qualities, and so on ad infinitum. A plant, to use Hegel's illustration, continually transcends its limitations of being a seed, a blossom, fruit, leaf, branch, and so forth. It must be noted, however, that in this negation qualities do not vanish as such but have a sublated subsistence within a new qualitative determination. As Hegel conceived qualitative transition, however, it was not a completely unmediated dissolution of one thing into another; rather a quality is transformed or altered into something hitherto external to itself, and yet an integral part of its former reality remains. This conception of quality as something distinct itself, as well as extraneous and separate from its own frontier, is an indispensable distinction underlying Hegel's ontology in general and the movement of quantity into quality in particular.

What has been said thus far of Hegel's notion of being follows directly from the essential character of quality: every determinate being must possess a particular and original wholeness or self-identity. It has been shown that this qualitative way of understanding consists of recognizing that otherness and self-sameness are participants in the same relation. To understand the difference between quality and quantity, however, it is essential that we begin to see objects in terms of units expressed in symbolic or numerical values, for the essential content of quantitative understanding is the introduction of units that can be made the objects of calculation. Thus instead of determining the inherent nature of an object of investigation, we are now concerned with determining the number of items that such objects or "ones" present to us. To be sure, Hegel deals with simple ones abstracted from any kind of inner diversity. There is just an externally related multiplicity of objects, determined as simply ones (or units).

Hegel's account of quantity starts out identical to Spinoza's distinction between the limitless and limited nature of pure quantity. The realization of quantity at first is an abstraction possessing no inner differentiation. We could say that at this point quantity is boundless, incoherent, and never joining with itself in its movement into other than itself. It is empty, so to speak, or simply a "bad infinite" as Hegel called it. Pure quantity "is not bounded by limit but, on the contrary, consists precisely in not being bounded by limit, in having [quality's] being-for-self within it as a sublated moment."[36] In this sense, pure quantity is completely independent of any number relation due to its noetic character. As homogeneous, it defies partitioning into fractional parts. We often think of space, time, the will, and the ego itself in terms of indivisible, limitless expansions that contain no opposites or barriers. Hegel, however, is not content with bad infinities of endless progress; he goes on to indicate that there really is no concrete example of pure quantity, for it is quantity as yet undetermined, and whatever is undetermined is pure being and thus identical to nothing. Hence eventually we come to view space and time as divisible (into places, feet, inches, and into ages, years, hours, minutes, respectively). Further, we envisage the will as the ego determined (and thus limited) in its activity. Indeed the will and the ego are self-limited or self-determinate for Hegel and thus not limitless.

For Hegel, as for Aristotle, quantity is both related and indifferent to quality.[37] Moreover, quantity is founded not merely qua quantity (that is, as a number independent of its object) but also involves "discrete" and "continuous" magnitude, which makes it determinate. Discrete magnitude is simply the idea that the "ones" or objects are different from one another. It presents us with different units (and not simply one huge unit or a heap), which in themselves are cut off from one another. Continuous magnitude, on the other hand, is the idea that the units are all ultimately identical qua units. Both discrete and continuous magnitude are complementary moments of quantity as such; that is, in order to decide a quantity within a particular limit, both parts stand in need of recognition. For instance, insofar as the space a ship occupies is made up of various cubic feet, we have many cubic feet, each of which occupies a different place from its neighbor, so in one respect each is different and thus discrete. But insofar as each is essentially a cubic foot, each is also identical and thus continuous. This concept holds true with the passengers on a ship as well. Each passenger is a different passenger from the others and hence a discrete magnitude, and each is also qua passenger identical, so we have continuous magnitude. This particular identity in difference is not hard to discern, but this is not the case with Hegel's rather ambiguous presentation of quantity as indifferent and external.

From Hegel's point of view, quantitative reckonings treat objects simply as units or "ones" and are obtained by abstracting from sensuous determinations and from quality per se. Quantity, which treats of many objects as each a unit, a simple "one," also operates under great flexibility before dimensionality is superseded. Accordingly, within the sphere of quantity, an object may be increased or diminished a certain amount and still remain what it is. Here, Hegel suggests, the unlimitedness of units of measure remains indifferent to the nature and boundaries of a quality. A quantitative change in a house, says Hegel, is of no immediate significance to the thing, as such. Hegel's reasoning here, however, is liable to error. Whereas in reality a house is a house is a house, if we reduce it enough, it becomes a doll's house or toy, and its nature is affected greatly by a quantitative alteration. Therefore things cannot augment and diminish, more or less, and still remain what they are.

The problem in determining objects from only a quantitative point of view immediately arises: when, for instance, is a body of water a puddle instead of a pond and vice versa? Hegel foresaw this predicament and warned against proceeding to comprehend objects quantitatively; the difficulty lies in understanding "their peculiar, that is their qualitative character."[38] Elsewhere he remarks that quantity is "a form of difference that does not touch the essential nature . . . does not attain to essential opposition or unlikeness; and hence involves no transition of one opposite element into its other, no qualitative, immanent movement, no self-movement."[39]

When quantity "appears distinguished or limited," that is, as a finite determination, it is at the stage of development of the Idea called *quantum*.[40] The chief characteristic of *quantum* (how much) emerges, we may suggest, from the problematic set forth in Plato's *Philebus*: how is it possible to conceive of the one as a plurality and a unity at the same moment?[41] Plato's account of bringing the indeterminateness of multiplicity within discernible limits proceeded by means of the example of music and of mathematics. Every sound, for instance, remains undelimited until it is brought within intelligible parameters through the agency of tonal factors. *Quantum* thus represents a definite amount; so considered as a unified assemblage of several properties, it constitutes a crystallization of itself. But even this specific value, at one moment elevated to a harmonious note, fluctuates, and its specific determinateness is thereby set aside.

A profound difference between the classical image of magnitude and Hegel's appraisal lies in the latter's novel element of necessity, which emerges as the result of his notion of the "infinite quantitative progression." Every *quantum* is a progressive self-development that always pushes out and beyond itself in a manner that defies repetition and reduction: "A quantum, therefore, in accordance with its quality, is posited in absolute continuity with its externality, with its otherness. Therefore, not only can it transcend every quantitative determinateness, not only can it be altered, but it is posited that it *must* alter."[42] In other words, as a quantity intensifies or decreases, it reaches its limits of development, at which point its self-realized character lies "outside it in other magnitudes."[43] From Hegel's standpoint, the Pythagorean conception that things are constituted in only number—"the being of all things is number"—was simply half-true; saying that 1 is basic, 2 is multiplicity, and 3 the coalescence of the former two is merely to express the external association of these numbers.[44] There remains nothing intrinsic that would connect them to either objects of sense or thought. The ontology of the Pythagoreans rests merely upon the possibility of the countableness of things, without ever disclosing their necessary connection.

The Hegelian notions of quality and quantity may be said to differ insofar as the former has the attributes of independence, stability, and peculiarity, whereas quantity is the expression of relativity, change, and variability. Ultimately the dialectic reveals how their separation and distinction, in its one-sidedness, breaks down and posits their mediate relation. This crucial movement results in what Hegel refers to as the moment of "measure." It is the specific link, the most explicit unity of quantity and quality, and "is thus the completion of Being."[45] Surely this movement is the creative feature of Hegel's dialectic, and yet in some respects it is perhaps one of Hegel's most slippery transitions.

Much of the confusion surrounding Hegel's transformation of quantity into quality has been due to subsequent analyses that have been either misleading or remarkably remote from the original conceptualization. This becomes clear when one encounters some commonly held assertions: quantitative changes *cause* or *pass* into, or *lead* to qualitative changes, as if the two terms are distinct and unassimilated. But let us first look at the groundwork of Hegel's own claim in the greater *Logic*:

the alterations of being in general are not only the transition of one magnitude into another, but a transition from quality into quantity and vice versa, a becoming-other which is an interruption of gradualness and the production of something qualitatively different from the reality which preceded it.[46]

Hegel here is expressing two very important distinctions that underlie the substance of the transition he is concerned with. First, we are dealing with two different measures that stand in relation to each other and will be converted into a reciprocal measure. Hence quality and quantity are never severed, nor are they distinctly independent actualities. According to Hegel, we have to overcome this *one-sided assumption of quantity* disappearing when it goes beyond its limit. In order to understand the transition properly, it must be viewed figuratively as, to use Hegel's terminology, a "manifold interrelationship" or "combination with other measures," both qualitative and quantitative aspects being determined at the same moment interchangeably. Second, this transition is a dynamic leap: it is a transgression of a specific threshold in contrast to a progressively gradual alteration. It is a "sudden interruption," when a "nodal" point of measure is finally passed. As such it is obscure in the sense that the dividing line (except in empirical science) is never pinpointed. It is only in the exact sciences that the measure in a nodal scale can be posited and specified with accuracy. In spheres such as morality, war, crime, and social systems, the point beyond which the determinancy of a new object begins is purely problematic; there is no decisive, predictable specification that can be fixed as a posited realization.

Meanwhile Hegel attempts to free quantitative distinctions from being rendered totally inconceivable. Within certain quantitative limits, he suggests, there may exist vacillations that manifest different proportions without ever affecting the quality or boundaries of a thing. In fact, we have encountered this dilemma elsewhere; for instance, in Greek literature the distinction is made between a horse with a bald tail and one with either one or a few hairs, and one of the fables concerns a donkey who collapsed after a certain weight was added to its load. But for Hegel these were problematics to the ancients only because such features were put forward as removed from their qualitative whole—that is, as independent of the self-subsistent totality: "The real mistake is committed by . . . assuming a quantity to be only an indifferent limit, i.e. of assuming that it is just a quantity in the specific sense of quantity. This assumption is refuted by the truth to which it is brought—to wit, that quantity is a moment of measure and is connected with quality."[47] Again, the issue is establishing precise limits, without which all measure of given qualities becomes relative. To be sure, it seems that such a positive definition that clearly sets forth parameters for each measure in the macroworld is unavailable. The deficiency of quantitative formulations continues to be their vagueness unless we deal with quantities and qualities as mutually dependent on each other.

Hegel's approach to the transitionary principle of quantity into quality appears metaphorical at times and more often as an undertaking in logic or pure thought. But he did distinguish various ways in which this notion presents itself in everyday life.

Quantitative arrangements embody greater potential changes in latitude and are ultimately more flexible than are qualitative substances. Simply by virtue of the fact that a quantity points beyond itself, a determination (fixed) of its limit remains contingent and arbitrary. Now we come face to face with the indeterminateness of quantitative relations when we enter the sphere of punishment. In attempting to fix punishments for crimes, judicial bodies are obliged to establish an equilibrium between punishments and offenses. The value of punishment an individual offender receives must be proportionate to the criminal act itself in some way. But the leeway peculiar to quantitative features prevents this from ever being stabilized into specific (positive) scales. The Benthamite precepts designed to establish fixed standards of punishment are utterly ineffective for this very reason.[48]

In the *Philosophy of Right* Hegel discusses at length the incoherence of any system that attempts to hold fast to inherently contingent elements in law:

Reason cannot determine, nor can the concept provide any principle whose application could decide whether justice requires for an offence (i) a corporal punishment of forty lashes or thirty-nine or (ii) fine of five dollars or four dollars ninety-three, four etc., cents, or (iii) imprisonment of a year or three hundred and sixty-four, three, etc., days, or a year and one, two or three days. And yet injustice is done at once if there is one lash too many, or one dollar or one cent, one week in prison or one day, too many or too few.[49]

In the *Science of Logic* Hegel brings this problem to the fore insofar as the transitionary principle is concerned. Here he states that "it is through a more and less that the measure of frivolity or thoughtlessness is exceeded and something quite different comes about, namely crime, and thus right becomes wrong and virtue vice."[50] Corrective justice, therefore, cannot be prescribed beyond a loose and general standard if it is to function well. Thus the value or magnitude of punishment must always remain relative according to the extent of harmfulness inflicted, for on its own account punishment always shuns ready-made yardsticks and must rest content with chance and indeterminacy. More than this, if we want unchanging and immutable standards of administration, is to pursue an unattainable goal.

Although Hegel's main concern here is to show the infeasibility of reducing punishment to exact proportions, yet he furnishes one important exception to the hypothetical way in which punishment must be meted out. In the case of murder, according to Hegel, we are in a position to decide the genuine value of a crime quite separate from the relativity of numerical relations. Hegel is, to be sure, unequivocal in his acceptance of capital punishment for crimes of murder, but it is not on any moral grounds that he reaches this conclusion. While all other crimes can be punished with reference to arithmetical knowledge (according to multitude), murder can be treated only in respect of kind. The reason, says Hegel, "is that since life is the full compass of a man's existence, the punishment here cannot simply consist in a 'value', for none is great enough, but can consist only in taking away a second life."[51] Here, too, Hegel is applying the central notion of a leap—from distinguishing crimes quantitatively to an exclusively qualitative distinction. It is only when crime reaches an excess that it can no longer be taken as a "more" or "less" and punished accordingly. In the case of murder, however, Hegel discerns that in actual fact a nodal point has been superseded by virtue of which the criminal can be punished only in such a way.

Hegel's conception of war treats quantitative determinations in a somewhat different manner, although his remarks on the subject are condensed and somewhat inconclusive.[52] They should be approached in the light of his theory of state activity in general.[53]

But one aspect of Hegel's position on the nature of war is that we can never lose sight of the decisive importance of quantitative determinations. Accordingly it is absurd to speak of a merely contingent connection between numerical considerations of an armed force and the outcome of a war itself. Strength of imagination, degree of motivation, extent of territory, and size of army may all be assessed according to "differences of intensity," which thus lend themselves a quantitative character. Certainly it is possible to view Hegel's argument that war is a difference of quantitative values as apparent nonsense. This may be the case, however, if one assumes that Hegel has in mind only progressively increasing scales of measure—that is, for example, an excessively large assemblage of troops wherein the force of numbers alone overpowers an enemy. But Hegel avoids this implausible argument. Once we consider quantitative distinctions in war, he says, we may envisage an inverse ratio occurring, and this would lead to the defeat of a great empire by even a considerably meager number of persons. The history of warfare well illustrates this point of view. The Greek defeat of Persia (490 B.C.), Hannibal's devastating victory (218 B.C.), and Napoleon's remarkable defeat of the Austrians (1800) all demonstrate instances in which the few conquered the many.[54]

The Applicators of Social Quantities

Let us recall briefly the underlying assertions of the so-called distinctive tradition, which has emerged in the course of the development of political discovery. In contrast to those authors who take their cue mainly from dialectics and who seek an understanding of the internal connection and mutual relatedness of the terms quantity and quality, the new school generally is concerned less with general determinations of the character of the notions as uniformities than with emphasizing their most immediate presentation and visible embodiment. To a large extent, their starting point has been a polemic against the classical or speculative construction of the terms as they search for a much more tangible, scientific use of the terms to explain facts of experience. Again and again, one finds in the theorists I discuss here this concern for a practical application of the categories often used exclusive from one another. Finally, quantity itself seems to become a predominant view and is regarded as specifically realized in the form of social power. Bacon, Hobbes, Petty, Bentham, Mill, and Marx, among others, all have in common this intimate concern with applicability and present the terms as determinate through a particular method.

Although Sir William Petty was not the first to apply quantitative points of view to government, he was one of the most powerful adherents of this mode of presenting human affairs as mathematical facts. It was the clarity and accuracy of mathematical cognition that led him to conclude, "There is a Political Arithmetic and a Geometrical Justice to be yet further cultivated in the world; the Errors and

Defects whereof, neither Wit, Rhetoric, nor Interest can more than palliate, never cure."[55] Closely related to Petty's belief that social facts were things that could be verified by observation and ultimately employed as a demonstrative rule was the method whereby he collected his data and drew together his observations. He says:

The Method I take to do this is not yet very usual; for instead of using only comparative and superlative Words, and intellectual Arguments, I have taken the course (as a Specimen of the Political Arithmetick I have long aimed at) to express myself in Terms of Number, Weight, or Measure; to use only Arguments of Sense.[56]

But the prevalent tendency within Petty's quite calculative works is the idea that the civil state is a whole proportion. From this it follows that the "wealth" and "strength" (objects that Petty was primarily concerned with) of a nation can be depicted in quantitative terms. In order to show this, Petty required some raw material for his studies besides logic and the propositions of metaphysics. Hence he was led to consider specifiable social facts, such as poll taxes, size and productiveness of land, annual consumption, surplus value, and size of the population. Petty himself could not draw upon many of the statistics now publicly provided. Indeed he was a pioneer in advocating such developments as a public census, which in Great Britain was not carried out until 1801. For this reason, many of his judgments were imprecise, but the ground he laid—in addition to some of his contemporaries and predecessors such as John Graunt and Gregory King—for vital statistics, revenue calculations, and even modern demography was itself a considerable achievement and has since gained wide currency. Indeed John Graunt's observations, "some concerning Trade and Government, others concerning the Air, Countries, Seasons, Fruitfulness, Health, Diseases, Longetivity, and the properties between the Sex and Ages of Mankind," comprise to a large extent the dimensions of demographical explanation.[57] The point I want to emphasize, however, is that political arithmetic and utilizing quantitative material about individual and social behavior constituted an important point of departure for political study.

In particular, political arithmetic provided a sound principle to guide decision making in matters related to war. It would be absurd to enter into a war without having first regarded the strength of one's enemy. But hitherto such judgments had been based on conjecture and thus were prone to error. Hence Petty demonstrated to Charles II, by way of figures, that the population of England was roughly equal to that of France, that England had only slightly less territory than its rival, and that England had more foreign trade per capita than did France.[58] "By contemplating the universal posture of the nation, its power, strength, trade, wealth and revenues . . . by summing up the difficulties on either side, and by computing upon the whole . . . is what we mean by Political Arithmetic."[59]

According to Petty, the whole body politic is based on a variety of purely material relations that, however extensive or limited, are nevertheless measurable in terms of ratios, means, and other mathematical yardsticks. At the same time, Petty never sees other relations of a less material nature that sustain and promote a nation's activities, such as morals, customs, attitudes, and extent of participation in government. All of these factors, though in less measurable terms, might be said to contribute to any determination of the strength of a political association yet fall outside his purview.

Prior to Bentham, the most strategic figure who sought to translate morals into quantitative formulas was the Scottish philosopher, Francis Hutcheson. In his *An Inquiry into the Origins of Our Ideas of Beauty and Virtue*, Hutcheson subjects moral judgments to a straightforward mathematical investigation. And although his venture is trite and rather crude, it nevertheless affords an insight into the practical mission and predominantly quantitative focus of his efforts. He attempted to fashion a mathematical morality:

1. The moral Importance of any Agent, or the Quantity of public Good produced by him, is in a compound Ratio of his Benevolence and Abilities: or (by substituting the initial Letters for the Words, as M= Moment of Good, and μ = Moment of Evil) $M = B \times A$.
2. In like Manner, the Moment of private Good, or Interest produced by a Person to himself, is in a compound Ratio of his Self-Love, and Abilities: or (substituting the initial Letters) $I = S \times A$.
3. When in comparing the virtue of two Actions, the Abilities of the Agents are equal; the Moment of public Good produced by them in like Circumstances, is as the Benevolence: or $M = B \times I$.

4. When Benevolence in two Agents is equal, and other Circumstances alike, the Moment of public Good is as the Abilities: or $M = A \times I$.

5. The Virtue then of Agents, or their Benevolence, is always directly as the Moment of Good produced in like Circumstances, and inversely as their

$$\text{Abilities: or } B = \frac{M}{A} \ .$$

6. But as the natural Consequences of our Actions are various, some good to ourselves, and evil to the Public; and others evil to ourselves, and Good to the Public; or either useful both to ourselves and others . . . but in most Actions we must look upon Self-Love as another Force, sometimes conspiring with Benevolence, and assisting it, when we are excited by Views of Private Interest, as well as public Good; and sometimes opposing Benevolence, when the good Action is any way difficult or painful in the Performance, or detrimental in its Consequences to the Agent. In the former case, $M = B + S \times A = BA + SA$, and therefore $BA = M - SA = M - I$, and

$$B = \frac{M - I}{A} . \text{ In the latter case,}$$

$$M = B - S \times A = BA - SA; \text{ therefore}$$
$$BA = M + SA = M + I, \text{ and } B = \frac{M + I}{A}.[60]$$

In an elaborate way, Hutcheson goes on to abbreviate even moral evil into a mathematical sequence. His work is significant not because it clarified the concepts of good and evil associated with moral decisions but because he was the first thinker to express moral dilemmas from a quantitative point of view. By means of this retransformation of the qualitative and symbolized content of moral questions, Hutcheson aimed at a purely fixed and regulated method of analysis.

The quantitative construct described here is not unique in the history of thought. The Hobbesian belief that "all men calculate," Petty's conceptualizations of a political association based on activities that could be weighed, measured, and reduced to common denominators, and Hutcheson's penchant for ready-made moral formulas are all present in Bentham. In the light of these positions, Bentham announces that moral, political, and religious judgments may be determined according to a simple working hypothesis, best known as the "felicific calculus." And although it is true that Bentham claims a lot for his hedonic formula, it must be seen together with his belief that the purpose of the state is to augment the happiness of its individuals and diminish pain and insecurity. Bentham even maintained that this was something more than a moral postulate that legislators ought to pursue. It was, in fact, nothing but a new version of a time-worn principle of political thought: that the basic schemata of a political state unfolded under an intrinsic concept or *telos*, which, in Bentham's case, referred exclusively to the idea of the greatest happiness of the community. It is, he points out, the "sole standard" or measure by which both general and particular laws can be understood.

Bentham's adherence to an ultimate goal and to the irrefutable elements of mathematics had an unmistakable practical foundation. As such, his calculations were not total in the sense of identifying once and for all the precise movement, relations, and conditions of society performed (or contained) within the felicific construct. Rather the Benthamite hedonic calculus was meant to be a generalized account and technique, a set of rules and assumptions, from which further occurrences of social life could be judged and calculated. As he says in the preface to *Principles of Morals and Legislation*, it "exhibited a set of propositions . . . affording a standard for the operations performed by government, in the creation and distribution of propriety and other civil rights."[61]

We can reconstruct briefly Bentham's account of measuring the quantity of value of pleasure in the following way. The value of pleasure or pain may be regarded under two relevant categories: the individual by himself and the community. These categories, however, are not entirely removed from one another. The content of the former depends on six factors: intensity, duration, certainty, propinquity, purity (distinctness from its opposite), and fecundity (reproduction of itself). But in order to measure an act within the latter category, it is necessary to include the six values in addition to extent (the number of persons affected by the act). The so-called objective sum now can be ascertained.

First, we add up the values of all of the pleasures and repeat the process for pains. If the balance is oriented toward the pleasurable situation, this may be considered a good act. If the scheme is overwhelmingly on the side of pain, we will be directed away from it in the future. The final account consists of transforming the procedure for the single person to the group and deciding in the same way whether the act or judgment is warranted for the good of the larger unit, or society.

The span of Bentham's measurement of the greatest good extends over a variety of social norms and institutions, such as behavioral explanations, moral sanctions, and legal systems. It must suffice to deal here with Bentham's recommendations on penal reform, especially inasmuch as they reveal a strong preoccupation with the terms *quantity* and *quality*.

Happiness of the kind Bentham speaks of presupposes the security of, at best, the moral and physical forces within states and, at least, the physical conditions of life. Laws are designed, suggests Bentham, to "inculcate principles" or instructions that shall benefit individuals with both the moral and physical ends in view. Offenses of laws are unavoidable; thus punishments need to be detailed according to the crime but prior to the criminal act itself. And although all crimes cannot be accounted for a priori, it is, as Bentham reminds us, of considerable utility to establish some sort of penal code. The most appropriate rule that treats infringements of the law in such a way that it outweighs the benefit or profit derived from the criminal act itself, and at the same time suitably guards against its being committed again, is to punish in greater proportion to the crime in question. As Bentham makes evident, "For the sake of quality, increase in quantity." And again, "the quality [of punishment] will be regulated by the quantity."[62] This includes considerations of the intensity and duration of punishment; the same currency may also render effective a "moral lesson," which seeks its reality in individual members of the community instead of the criminal. Bentham is concerned less with the prevention of offenses (a causalist attitude toward crime) than establishing a maxim whereby the proportion between punishment and crime can be recognized and applied consistently.

Regardless of how fruitless Bentham's rules of social measurement may seem, they point to the fact that political cognition had become bound up in a mathematical attitude that aimed at regularity, fixed conceptions, and measurable phenomena. As such, it became a driving force in remaking the occupation of political knowledge.

Francis Edgeworth, in his *Mathematical Psychics: An Essay on the Application of Mathematics to the Moral Sciences*, attempts to apply the precise formulations of mathematics a stage further than Bentham. Neither the application of mathematics to public opinion nor the use of statistical techniques in physics satisfied Edgeworth. "The calculus of Feeling, of Pleasure and Pain" and even what he called "the application of mathematics to the world of soul" became his primary study.[63]

Edgeworth's unbounded enthusiasm for quantitative explanations of individual and social behavior is evidenced early in his *Mathematical Psychics* where he remarks, "The science of quantity is not alien to the study of man . . . in so far as actions and effective desires can be *numerically* measured by way of statistics."[64] Elsewhere he set forth a belief widely held by later political scientists: "He that will not verify his conclusions as far as possible by mathematics, as it were bringing the ingots of common sense to be assayed and coined at the mint of the sovereign science, will hardly realize the full value of what he holds, will want a measure of what it will be worth in however slightly altered circumstances, a means of conveying and making it current."[65]

Edgeworth's measurement endeavors rest on three underlying assumptions. The first is that all social relationships and subjective states of consciousness contain "precise data." There is little doubt that Edgeworth sought to have the best of two worlds—mathematics and psychology—by reducing and translating all subjective states and social differences to commensurable degrees or, as he called them, "perceivable instruments."

Second, for Edgeworth, large-scale social phenomena share the same properties as do physical forces. In looking at the political prism, Edgeworth saw uniformities of price and time-intensity units of pleasure and pain as analogous to such mechanical properties as the indefinite divisibility of matter and the accumulation (time-integral) of energy.

"Mécanique sociale" and "mécanique celeste" were logically inseparable to Edgeworth inasmuch as both were ultimately governed by the supreme "maximum principle": "The principal inquiries in Social Science may be viewed as *maximum-problems*. For Economics investigates the arrangements between agents each tending to his own *maximum* utility; and Politics and (Utilitarian) Ethics investigate the arrangements which conduce to the maximum sum total of utility."[66]

The third assumption that Edgeworth uncritically accepted in formulating his mathematical ethics was that man is by nature a "pleasure machine."[67] The impulse that drives individuals and that springs up between people is the strictly hedonic quest for unshaken sensual happiness. This notion, to be sure, is partly no more than a restatement of Bentham's "greatest happiness of the greatest number."

Fundamentally the object of political science according to Edgeworth (and all important to utilitarian thought) is "to find the distribution of means and of labor, the quality and number of population, so that there may be the greatest possible happiness."[68] By "pleasure" Edgeworth means "preferable feeling" and, conversely, the "absence of pain." "Means" apply to the production process and the consequent gain of wealth for comfortable living or as a "means" of exchange. The maximization of pleasure units for the happiness of one individual will vary with that of another. In other words, the "capacity for happiness," in a strictly utilitarian world guided by the law of "unequal distribution," will be proportional to the amount of means one can acquire in the public realm and also by the means (or talents) of an individual. There are no equals in the logarithmic mean process. As a result, so-called equal opportunity of means goes hand in hand with a very striking inequality of condition.

The concrete meaning of Edgeworth's doctrine of capacity for happiness is that individuals and social groups will remain unequal due to natural differences in talents and abilities and because wealth inheritance (enrichment of means) was a basic inequality transmitted through social organization. As Edgeworth puts it, "Capacity for pleasure is a property of evolution, an essential attribute of civilization. . . . To lower classes was assigned the work for which they seemed most capable; the work of the higher classes being different in kind was not to be equated in severity."[69]

In order to distinguish the formula of the greatest possible happiness from Bentham, Edgeworth adopted an axiomatic format similar to that found in Newton's *Principiia Mathematica*. His six postulates are:

1. The rate of increase of pleasure decreases as its means increase.

2. The rate of increase of fatigue increases as the work done increases.

3. The capacity for pleasure and capacity for work generally speaking go together . . . they both rise with evolution.

4. As population increases, means . . . increase at a decreasing rate.

5. To substitute in one generation for any number of parents an equal number each superior in capacity (evolution) is beneficial for the next generation.

6. To substitute in one generation for any number of parents an equal number each superior in capacity (evolution) is beneficial for all time.[70]

Two new happiness formulas emerge from these postulates. The first pertains to the "happiness of the present generation"; the second is supposed to be of predictive value inasmuch as it pertains to "the happiness of the next generation."

$$\int_{x_0}^{x_1} n[F(xy) - cy] \, dx + cD$$

$$H^1 = \int_{-\alpha}^{+\alpha} [n^1(F(xy) - cy)] \, dx + cD,$$

where x = degree of capacity for either happiness or work,

n = number of individuals,

x_1, x_0 = maximum and minimum capacities for pleasure,

$F(xy)$ = a unit's pleasure of consumption,

c = a relative maximum,

y = an individual's means,

D = the given distribution of means and labor,

OC = the greatest extent of variation,

N^1 = the capacities of the next generation,

H^1 = the happiness of the next generation.

Two consequences follow from Edgeworth's formula making. First, the happiness and comfort of some of the lower classes in society may have to be sacrificed for the advantage of other, higher classes. Edgeworth does point out that there is a bottom line, "the starvation point," beyond which political instability occurs and the grand aristocratic values of society grind to some political axe.

As for the second consequence, Edgeworth's formula suggests that the maximum capacities for pleasure and consumption activities may have to be sacrificed for future generations. Further analysis, however, shows that the Edgeworthian notion of sacrifice, far from being universal in application, really aims at restricting the reproduction of so-called lower-capacity individuals. Through this pernicious brand of selective deprivation, Edgeworth sought to improve the quality of population growth by forbidding the poor to be born.

But we must move on in our elucidation of the terms *quantity* and *quality*. Although it may seem out of place to introduce Marx at this point, nevertheless the transition of quantity to quality is a key notion in his political philosophy. And our understanding of his use of this notion perhaps may benefit from an analysis of why he appears in this practico-applicator, as opposed to a theoretical, context.

Looking back briefly to the criteria that critically differentiate distinctive from oppositional modes of presentation, we note that there exists a real break and shift of emphasis; in the distinctive analyses, a special concern for practical demonstration is clearly evident. Instead of emphasizing the sufficient logical conditions or theoretical basis of the terms, this emphasis on *praxis* and activity is fundamental to Marx's approach to the subject matter. We see this illustrated in his doctoral thesis on Greek atomism where he says that "it is a psychological law that once the theoretical intellect has achieved freedom within itself it turns into practical energy."[71] This is apparent also in the second *Thesis on Feuerbach*. Marx insists here that "the question of whether objective truth can be attributed to human thinking is not a question of theory but is a practical question."[72]

Marx, then, is focusing his attention on the practical and empirical involvement of the principles of quantity and quality.[73] The question that remains is how he applied the two terms and the ways in which they were illustrated in a practical context.

A starting point is to recall what perhaps is the fullest discussion of the basic character of quantity and quality and their relation to one another—that developed by Hegel. There it became clear that the dynamic transition from a quantitative to a qualitative state is reached when a nodal point of measure is finally passed. Marx took up this Hegelian idea and reconstructed it with "the materialist conception of history." Thus when we come across the declaration, such as that found in the *Contribution to the Critique of Hegel's Philosophy of Right* to the effect that "as the determined adversary of the previous form of German political consciousness, the criticism of the speculative philosophy of right does not remain within its own sphere, but leads on to tasks which can only be solved by means of practical activity," this does not mean that Marx rejected Hegel's categories.[74] Rather he argued that they can be understood only from the "active-life process" of history. The "transformation of history into world history," Marx observes, "is by no means a mere abstract act on the part of 'self consciousness,' the world spirit, or of any other metaphysical spectre, but a quite material, empirically verifiable act, an act the proof of which every individual furnishes as he comes and goes, eats, drinks and clothes himself."[75]

For Marx, then, insofar as the transition from quantity to quality is concerned, standing Hegel on his feet was less a problem than demonstrating the historical manner in which this conceptualization is actually satisfied. Marx's main aim was thus to develop Hegel's discovery by filling its abstract or speculative character with the reality of the concrete and finite determinations of history. The task of our newly won Hegelian knowledge, as Marx puts it in the *Grundrisse*, is not "the dialectical balancing of concepts"; rather it is "the grasping of real relations."[76]

From Marx's position, the first place where this formative change occurs is in the breakdown of medieval production and the consequent transition to capitalist production:

Manufacture, in its strict meaning, is hardly to be distinguished, in its earliest stages, from the handicraft trades of the guilds, otherwise than by the greater number of workmen simultaneously employed by one and the same individual capital. The workshop of the medieval mast handicraftsman is simply enlarged. At first, therefore, the difference is purely quantitative.[77]

To begin with, then, Marx expresses the economic transition into capitalism as an increase of quantitative features beyond a certain limit: from the one-man or small-group guild workshop to the much later developed and significantly enlarged capitalist factory.

Marx envisioned that this transition from feudal landownership and the feudal organization of trade to fully developed capitalist production was a long drawn-out process that took several centuries to mature. Marx repeatedly notes that the transition from serf to journeyman to industrial laborer occurred very gradually; this almost seems the most appropriate motto of precapitalist development. In the *German Ideology* Marx suggests that the bourgeois class "arose only gradually" out of the local corporations of burghers in the Middle Ages.[78] And in the first volume of *Capital*, Marx notes that the whole development of the manufacturing period of capitalism, which led to the domination of the world market by England, lasted for over two centuries.[79]

The actual character of the transition was by no means uniform and contained a wealth of developmental variations in both time and place. This is a crucial feature of Marx's historical materialism and too often is neglected in evaluations of Marx simply in terms of economics or in criticisms of his general breakdown of socioeconomic epochs in the preface to *A Contribution to the Critique of Political Economy*. As Marx pointed out in the *Grundrisse*, "Between the full development of this foundation of industrial society and the patriarchal condition, many intermediate stages, endless nuances [occur]."[80]

The intelligibility of capitalist modes of production develops as we grasp the terrain of feudal institutions to which they belong. The fourteenth and fifteenth centuries witnessed the collapse of large-scale demesne farming and international trade. The period was marked by glutted labor markets and saw the creation of extensive slave economies in Africa, Europe, and the Americas.

The abolition of feudal agricultural arrangements in the countryside and guild handicraft production in the towns was an ongoing evolution. Time and again the feudal economic and social crises recovered, and the direct exploitation of labor sources by dint of feudal lordship or guild master rights continued. The replacement of labor rent with money rent illustrates just another way station on the long road to definitive capitalism.

In the last half of the eighteenth century, individual capitalists had displaced both guild masters and feudal lords. Serfs were emancipated and transformed into so-called free proletarians, who, according to Marx, found their masters waiting for them in the towns in the form of industrial "potentates." Manufacture and machine industry creates a greater division and specialization of labor and accentuates the production of large quantities of goods, which is closely linked with the growing accumulation of capital.

The specific tendency of capitalist production to appropriate a never-ending surplus of goods, which leads it to search after new and greater markets, excludes qualitative differences. Nonrepetitive actions, a close connection to the article produced in its final form, careful consideration of variable human abilities and needs, and better-made products of greater durability, detail, and aesthetic skill are some of the qualitative distinctions Marx had in mind.[81] Such changes as the development of technical, labor-saving machinery, the extension of the scale of capitalist production, or the consolidation of the processes of production are not qualitative constituents, for these so-called improvements in laboring methods are brought about at the expense of the laboring class. Regarding the purely quantitative character of capitalist accumulation, Marx says, "The law, finally, that always equilibrates the relative surplus-population, or industrial reserve army, to the extent and energy of accumulation, this law rivets the laborer to capital more firmly than the wedges of Vulcan did Prometheus to the rock. It establishes an accumulation of misery, corresponding with accumulation of capital."[82] In a word, "Time is everything, man is nothing, he is, at the most, time's carcase. Quality no longer matters. Quantity alone decides everything, hour for hour, day for day."[83]

We have thus far seen that the moment in which the full-fledged character of capitalism first expressed itself must be taken in a relative sense. Marx's concrete elucidation of Hegel's precepts is at once apparent in that the crystallization of the small master of the medieval workshop into a capitalist owner was an alteration of magnitude that changed the specific quality belonging to the guild system:

The possessor of money or commodities actually turns into a capitalist in such cases only where the maximum sum advanced for production greatly exceeds the maximum of the middle ages. Here, as in natural science, is shown the correctness of the law discovered by Hegel . . . that merely quantitative differences beyond a certain point pass into qualitative changes.[84]

If the law of transition from quantity to quality as witnessed in the emergence of capitalism has created the impression that Marx's formulation was somewhat nondefinitive, it must be remembered that this occasional allusive use of language is good Hegelianism. The Hegelian thesis, of course, held that the climax of any system, the point beyond which it is the determinancy of an object, is purely problematic; there is no decisive, predictable point at which the real movement can be said to occur. But Marx overlooks this in his references to the transformation of a socialist society subject to its own laws. Moreover, from Marx's vantage point, starting from the time he and Engels wrote *German Ideology* in 1845–1846, there is a sense of immediacy peculiar to the transformation of capitalism into a socialist world: "Empirically, communism is only possible as the act of the dominant people 'all at once' and simultaneously, which presupposes the universal development of productive forces and the world intercourse bound up with communism."[85] On closer examination we find that the special emphasis on the dialectical leap never appeared in Marx's evaluation of the earlier transition to capitalist society, while one finds it to be an important component of the emerging new socialist society.[86]

It is thus in the very novel approach to the category of the leap whose fundamental tenet is the fact of a significant crisis or violent struggle that dominates the course of social transition leading toward socialism that we find a shift of emphasis in Marx's writings. This shift was apparent from his earlier relevant writings to the analyses in *Capital*.

Some modern Marxians have developed the implications of this critical turning point or leap in history more radically than Marx himself had done. Typical of this line of reasoning is Lukács's conclusion that "each crisis signifies a deadlock in the ordered evolution of capitalism."[87] A point of greater significance is the assertion that every crisis or turn taken within the fundamental capitalist structure constitutes an "inevitable" and "imminent" movement toward the historical moment of transformation and liberation.[88] In this respect, Gramsci raised a highly relevant point: "assertions regarding periods of crisis or prosperity can give rise to one-sided judgements."[89] This in no way, however, explains the source of immediacy in Marx's penetration of Hegel's categories.

The essentially practical (revolutionary) component that Marx inserted into the problem of transition was less a product of his recognition that man is the subject-object of knowledge and accordingly reshapes his own reality than a result of the special emphasis he placed on the development of productive forces and, more specifically, on the accentuated character of the capitalist relations of production. This peculiar course of development, which made it possible to identify a decisive thrust (a violent and induced transition to socialism), was due to the law of capitalist accumulation. Ostensibly, however, we can trace Marx's preoccupation with the urgent termination of capitalist society to two economic and commercial crises that occurred in 1857 and 1866. According to Marx, these crises in the production of capitalist accumulation took on a financial character. Of central importance were the piling up of unsold goods, mounting bankruptcies, and a rapid rise in unemployment. In a letter, Marx portrayed the sense of immediacy that was such a keystone of his transitionary prospectus when he declared, "I am working like mad all through the nights at putting my economic studies together so that I may at least have the outlines clear *before the deluge comes*."[90]

A failure to come to grips on a formal level with the quantitative expansion of capital accumulation, which finally reaches its limit in expanding productivity and then, as Marx puts it, "bursts asunder," and, on a more immediate level, the actual developments which in part prompted Marx's enquiries, will doubtless lead to some type of bias or blindness in understanding Marx's reconstruction of the Hegelian idea of transition.[91] These two features combined opened the way for Marx's element of the leap from quantitative to qualitative relations between men.

We come now to the last figure to be represented under the category of distinction, Max Weber. Weber's approach to transitions is wholly different from those of Marx, whose emphasis was on the unilinear development of social history that progressed from feudalism to capitalism to the qualitatively new socialist society. In particular, according to Marx, the overproduction of capital and periodic crisis brought about by the anarchy of capitalist production hastened this transitionary process. Weber, on the other hand, does not assert, as Marx had, that history is marked by such clear-cut universal phases. As he put it, "Thus far the continuum of European culture development has known neither completed cyclical movements nor an unambiguously oriented 'unilinear development.' "[92] Accordingly, history for Weber does not exhibit any logical transitions that follow inevitably from each other. Yet Weber does suggest that one can find a fundamental characteristic in the *decursus vitae* of history, which he calls "bureaucratization."

Like Marx, Weber regarded the development of modern bureaucracy as closely bound up with the growth of industrialism. He stressed, however, the technical superiority that bureaucratic organization had over other forms of organization:

The fully developed bureaucratic apparatus compares with other organizations exactly as does the machine with the non-mechanical modes of production. Precision, speed, unambiguity, knowledge of the files, continuity, discretion, unity, strict subordination, reduction of friction and of material and personal costs—these are raised to the optimum point in the strictly bureaucratic administration.[93]

Weber also drew attention to the intimate connection between bureaucratic domination and the rise of capitalism:

Today, it is primarily the capitalist market economy which demands that the official business of public administration be discharged precisely, unambiguously, continuously, and with as much speed as possible. Normally, the very large modern capitalist enterprizes are themselves unequalled models of strict bureaucratic organization. Business management throughout rests on increasing precision, steadiness, and, above all, speed of operations.[94]

It is important to note one further element that Weber considered significant for modern bureaucracy: calculable rules and results. Rational calculation in the Western world, says Weber, first occurred in the seventeenth century, to a large extent due to capital accounting and especially to the introduction of double-entry bookkeeping. (Calvinism, and its ethical sanction for economic rationalism, for the entrepreneur, and for the spirit of craftsmanship, also contributed to methods of calculation and a rational business economy.)

By "bureaucratization" Weber means the "objective . . . discharge of business according to calculable rules and 'without regard for persons.' "[95] The general content of bureaucratic domination, however, Weber identifies with the principle of rationality: "By 'rationality' we here mean a force which promotes the orientation of economic activity of strata interested in purchase and sale of goods on the market to the market situations."[96] Taking for granted that bureaucratization and rational economic determination go hand in hand, we can proceed with Weber's distinction between quantity and quality, along with the quite specific ways these terms relate to bureaucracy and formal rationality.

For Weber, bureaucratization had two indispensable preconditions: the quantitative and the qualitative development of administrative tasks. What we have in the quantitative side of bureaucratic administration are extensive determinations, whereas the qualitative character of bureaucracy depends upon intensive features. Weber observes, "In politics, the big state and the mass party are the classic field of [quantitative] bureaucratization."[97] The ancient Roman Empire and the apparatus of party officials in the United States he labels prime examples of this conception of extensive bureaucratization. What is present in the case of the Roman Empire is a tendency to expand political frontiers. This required an immense standing army, which, until the reign of Diocletian in the third century, was easily mustered by the Republic. The consequences of a decline in the number of troops available to defend the frontiers were far-reaching. The import of party officialdom in the United States for Weber's notion of quantitative bureaucracy is an internally related matter. It is concerned with the decreasing frequency of voter independence, which in turn has led to control of party organization by professionals or political bosses. This group of inner-core politicians constitutes a major power block in nominating party candidates and has increasingly become, in Weber's words, a "social structure" in itself. Weber here, of course, is dealing with machine politics, to which he was personally averse but which he perceived as a further rationalization of the modern political process.

Although qualitative changes in bureaucracy do not necessarily follow or precede extensive development, it is nevertheless a more important determination for Weber. "Bureaucratization is stimulated more strongly," he says, "by intensive and qualitative expansion of the administrative tasks than by their extensive and quantitative increase."[98] Weber is careful to add that the actual changes of things with regard to intensive bureaucratization have varied widely over time. In other words, the "intensity of the administration" of, say, an ancient hydraulic society differs considerably from the management of a modern industrial enterprise.

What is peculiar to the qualitative development of bureaucracy is the underlying economic order, a principle Weber shared with Marx. "Increasing [qualitative] bureaucratization," he wrote, "is a function of the increasing possession of consumption goods, and of an increasingly sophisticated technique of fashioning external life—a technique which corresponds to the opportunities provided by such wealth."[99] Thus as distinguished from extensive officialdom, the main character of intensive (qualitative) administration is economic in general. This aspect of bureaucracy resolves itself into such matters as public finance, trade and communication, and social welfare policies. Moreover, it presupposes a certain level of rational calculation in the economy in kind or in money.

We have to distinguish, Weber suggests, among the different levels of economic transaction. In primitive societies, for instance, rational calculation is apparently absent. All that goes on here is hunting for food and the satisfaction of other essential human needs, such as clothing and shelter. There exist no institutions that rationally manage these activities and specialize in economic functions. Religious and/or military institutions embody, according to Weber, only a "very low level" of rationalization. Planned economies, however, and those where rationing of the means of production is introduced, bear a "very modest beginning of calculation."[100] The situation changes drastically in a system of money accounting, which, in terms of actively promoting rationality, is the highest form of calculation. Here the particular aspects of qualities are subordinated to efficient and objective calculations. In such cases, qualitatively different goods are compared and made identical through monetary valuations. Money accounting, therefore, is wholly nonqualitative. This is why Weber says that from a rational efficiency point of view "money is the most 'perfect' means of economic calculation." It provides, among other results, "the quantitative statement of (a) the expected advantages of every projected course of economic action and (b) the actual results of every completed action, in the form of an account comparing money costs and money returns and the net profit to be gained from alternatives of action."[101]

Having pointed out the peculiarities of a modern, bureaucratically institutionalized culture and the special kinds of connections involved in a specifically high-level or market economy, Weber states that his treatise has purposely avoided normative questions, such as whether the "monocratic" bureaucratic apparatus should be replaced by a planned economy. This sort of evaluative judgment, Weber rightly points out, cannot be made on scientific grounds.[102] Hence it is important not to be misled into supposing that Weber is carrying on a polemic against the conditions of bureaucracy as such. Thus far Weber is on firm ground.

But it is worthwhile to note that to a considerable extent his philosophical emphasis was positivistic in nature. It is not possible here to discuss the various dimensions of his methodological approach. I wish to stress only the overwhelming attention this conceptual framework pays to quantitative factors. And although Weber's perspective was distinguishingly broad, embracing historical, cultural, and developmental elements common to all human societies, his adherence to the method of empirical science meant an emphasis on quantity over quality. This can be seen, for example, in the following comment: "in the last analysis, all qualitative contrasts in reality can somehow be comprehended as purely quantitative differences made up of combinations of various single factors."[103] Elsewhere Weber is concerned to show that the specific evaluations one makes of social interconnections follows along the lines of a general approach in the natural sciences. This, so far as Weber is concerned, means the search for regularities attributable to human behavior from which empirical generalizations or types can be constructed: "It is possible in the field of social action to observe certain empirical uniformities. Certain types, that is, of action which correspond to a typically appropriate subjective meaning attributable to the same actors, are found to be widespread, being frequently repeated by the same individual or simultaneously performed by many different ones."[104] The upshot of this position was the formulation of a social understanding that claimed scientific efficacy and that accepted the conspectus of the exact sciences. In this respect, Weber was hardly different from the other thinkers we have examined.

Notes

1. Hobbes, *English Works*, ed. W. Molesworth (London, 1839), vol. 1, p. 2.

2. See, for example, Spinoza's *Tractatus Politicus* (1677): "My object in applying my mind to politics is . . . to investigate the topics pertaining to this branch of knowledge with the same objectivity as we generally show in mathematical inquiries." *The Political Works*, ed. A. G. Wernham (Oxford, 1958), p. 263.

3. See Plato, *Phaedo*, trans. Hugh Tredennick, in *Collected Dialogues*, ed. Edith Hamilton and Huntington Cairns (Princeton, 1973), 70e.

4. Plato, *Theaetetus*, trans. F. M. Cornford, in *Collected Dialogues*, 182b.

5. See Plato, *Philebus*, trans. R. Hackford, in *Collected Dialogues*, 24c.

6. Plato, *Republic*, trans. Paul Storey, in *Collected Dialogues*, 511c.

7. Plato, *Theaetetus*, 181d.

8. St. Thomas Aquinas, *Summa Theologica*, pt. 1, 2d rev. ed. (London, 1920), vol. 4, q. 85, art. 1, p. 186.

9. Plotinus, *The Enneads*, trans. Stephen MacKenna (London, 1956), fifth ennead, first tractate, p. 373.

10. See Robert Boyle, *The Origin of Forms and Qualities* (Oxford, 1666); and John Locke, *An Essay Concerning Human Understanding*, ed. Benjamin Rand (Cambridge, Mass., 1931).

11. At least by Aristotle. Aquinas's solution was to subdivide Aristotle's third and fourth type of sensibles into three classes: "Size, shape, and the like [he says], which are called *common sensibles*, are midway between *accidental sensibles* and *proper sensibles*, which are the objects of the sense. For the proper sensibles . . . are qualities that cause alteration. But the common sensibles are all reducible to quantity." *Summa Theologica*, vol. 4, q. 78, art. 3, p. 84.

12. Aristotle, *The Politics*, ed. Ernest Barker (Oxford, 1970), pp. 184–85.

13. Ibid., p. 185.

14. Ibid.

15. Aristotle, *Ethics*, trans. John Warrington (London, 1963), p. 35.

16. Aquinas, *Summa Theologica*, vol. 2, q. 42, art. 1, pp. 180–81.

17. Ibid., vol. 3, q. 52, art. 2, p. 27.

18. Immanuel Kant, *Critique of Pure Reason*, trans. J. M. D. Meiklejohn (London, 1934), p. 81.

19. Ibid., p. 73.

20. Ibid., p. 82.

21. Ibid., p. 122.

22. Ibid., p. 183.

23. Ibid., p. 131.

24. Kant, *Idea for a Universal History from a Cosmopolitan Point of View*, trans. Lewis W. Beck, in *On History*, ed. Lewis W. Beck (New York, 1963), p. 11.

25. Kant, *On the Foundation of Morality*, trans. Brendon E. Liddell (London, 1970), p. 192.

26. Ibid., p. 97.

27. Kant, *On History*, p. 140.

28. Ibid., p. 50.

29. Kant, *On the Foundation of Morality*, p. 50.

30. Kant, *Perpetual Peace*, ed. Lewis W. Beck (Indianapolis, 1957), pp. 44–45.

31. Kant, *On History*, p. 151.

32. Kant, *Perpetual Peace*, pp. 9–10.

33. *Hegel's Logic*, trans. William Wallace, 3d ed. (Oxford, 1975), sec. 85.

34. Hegel, *The Phenomenology of Mind*, trans. J. B. Baillie, 2d ed. (London, 1949), p. 113.

35. Hegel, *Science of Logic*, trans. A. V. Miller (London, 1969), p. 129.

36. Ibid., p. 188.

37. See Hegel, *Logic*, sec. 92; Aristotle, *Metaphysics*, 1020b.

38. Hegel, *Logic*, sec. 99.

39. Hegel, *Phenomenology of Mind*, p. 103.

40. Hegel, *Logic*, sec. 99.

41. See Plato, *Philebus*, 14c–17a; Hegel, *Phenomenology of Mind*, pp. 164ff.

42. Hegel, *Science of Logic*, p. 225.

43. Hegel, *Logic*, sec. 104.

44. See Aristotle, *Metaphysics*, 987a.

45. Hegel, *Logic*, sec. 107.

46. Hegel, *Logic*, p. 370.

47. Ibid., p. 336.

48. See Hegel, *The Philosophy of Right*, trans. T. M. Knox (Oxford, 1942), sec. 99, for Hegel's attack on utilitarian principles; see also David E. Cooper, "Hegel's Theory of Punishment" in *Hegel's Political Philosophy*, ed. Z. A. Pelczynski (Cambridge, 1971).

49. *Philosophy of Right*, sec. 214.

50. Hegel, *Science of Logic*, p. 371. The transition from interest to usury might be cited here as a more concrete instance of the transition from quantity to quality.

51. *Philosophy of Right*, sec. 101.

52. See ibid., sec. 324–50; *Phenomenology of Mind*, p. 497; and Constance I. Smith, "Hegel on War," in *Journal of the History of Ideas* 26 (1965).

53. See especially D. P. Verene, "Hegel's Account of War," in *Hegel's Political Philosophy*.

54. See H. A. L. Fisher, *A History of Europe* (London, 1936), pp. 27, 764, 830; Napthalin Lewis and Meyer Reinhold, *Roman Civilization* (New York, 1951), vol. 1, pp. 230–35; and Karl A. Wittfogel, *Oriental Despotism* (London, 1957), p. 63.

55. William Petty, *The Economic Writings of Sir William Petty*, ed. Charles Hull (New York, 1963), vol. 1, p. 240.

56. Ibid., p. 244.

57. See ibid., vol. 2, p. 232. See also Antoine de Montchiétien, *Traicté de l'oeconomie politique* (1615), one of the first textbooks on political economy to use statistical surveys in order to augment a political argument (in favor of a more equitable system of taxation).

58. One of Petty's disciples remarked, "Through the whole course of his writings may be plainly seen . . . that he was to advance a proposition, not quite right in itself, but very grateful to those who governed." Charles D'Avenant, *Political and Commercial Works* (London, 1971), vol. 1, p. 129.

59. Ibid., p. 135.

60. Francis Hutcheson, *An Inquiry into the Origins of Ideas from Beauty and Virtue*, 2d ed. (London, 1726), pp. 182–84 (with slight modifications in the spelling).

61. Jeremy Bentham, *An Introduction to the Principles of Morals and Legislation* (London, 1823), vol. 1, p. v.

62. Ibid., chaps. 14, xxii, p. 25 and 15, i, p. 33.

63. Francis Edgeworth, *Mathematical Psychics: An Essay on the Application of Mathematics to the Moral Sciences* (London, 1881), pp. 1, 9.

64. Ibid., p. 1.

65. Ibid., p. 3.

66. Ibid., pp. 6–7.

67. Ibid., p. 15.

68. Ibid., p. 56.

69. Ibid., pp. 77–78.

70. Ibid., pp. 61–71.

71. Karl Marx, *Early Texts*, ed. D. McLellan (Oxford, 1971), p. 15.

72. Marx, *Thesis on Feuerbach*, no. 2, quoted in John Hoffman, *Marxism and the Theory of Praxis* (London, 1975), p. 21.

73. Marx stressed the necessity to "bring out empirically . . . the connection of the social and political structures with production." Marx and Engels, *The German Ideology*, in *Collected Works* (London, 1976), vol. 5, p. 35. See also D. Livergood, *Marx's Philosophy of Action* (The Hague, 1967).

74. Marx, *Early Writings*, ed. T. B. Bottomore (London, 1964), p. 52.

75. Marx and Engels, *The German Ideology*, p. 51.

76. Marx, *Grundrisse* (Harmondsworth, Middlesex, 1973), p. 90. See also Marx, *The Poverty of Philosophy* (Moscow, 1955), p. 95.

77. Marx, *Capital* (New York, 1906), vol. 1, p. 353.

78. Marx, *German Ideology*, p. 77.

79. Marx, *Capital*, p. 369.

80. Marx, *Grundrisse*, p. 193. See also *Capital*, p. 787.

81. Marx, *Capital*, p. 401.

82. Ibid., p. 709.

83. Marx, *Poverty of Philosophy*, p 47.

84. Marx, *Capital*, pp. 337–38.

85. Marx, *German Ideology*, p. 49.

86. See ibid., pp. 34, 72.

87. Georg Lukács, *History and Class Consciousness* (London, 1971), p. 243.

88. Ibid., pp. 220, 250.

89. Antonio Gramsci, *The Modern Prince* (New York, 1957), p. 172.

90. Marx and Engels, *Selected Correspondence 1846–1895* (London, 1943), p. 225. Emphasis added.

91. See Marx, *Capital*, p. 837; *Grundrisse*, p. 706; and *Critique of Hegel's Philosophy of Right*, ed. Joseph O'Malley (Cambridge, 1977), p. 57.

92. Max Weber, "Agrageschicte des Altertums," *Handwörterbuch des Staatswissenschaften* (Jena, 1895–1897), vol. 1, p. 182, quoted in *From Max Weber*, ed. H. H. Gerth and C. Wright Mills (London, 1970), p. 51.

93. Weber, *Economy and Society*, ed. Guerther Roth and Claus Wittich (New York, 1968), vol. 3, p. 973.

94. Ibid., p. 974.

95. Ibid., p. 975.

96. Ibid., vol. 1, p. 84.

97. Ibid., vol. 3, p. 969.

98. Ibid., p. 971.

99. Ibid., p. 972.

100. Ibid., vol. 1, p. 107.

101. Ibid., p. 86.

102. Ibid., p. 112. Se also his *Methodology of the Social Sciences* (New York, 1949), p. 52.

103. Weber, *Religionssoziologie*, vol. 1, p. 265, quoted in *From Max Weber*, p. 59.

104. Weber, *The Theory of Social and Economic Development* (New York, 1947), pp. 120–21.

(2)

A Reassessment
of Bacon

> Nothing can be known
> completely except quantities
> or by quantities.
>
> —*Kepler*

Francis Bacon (1561–1626) the officeholder acquired nearly as many appellations as Francis Bacon the philosopher had friends and enemies. Queen Elizabeth called him her "young Lord Keeper" as he stood in the shadow of his father, Sir Nicholas Bacon, lord keeper of the Great Seal. In 1584 he became a member of Parliament, and soon afterward he began an ambitious career in the House of Lords. Under King James I, Bacon was appointed to the offices of solicitor general in 1607, attorney general in 1613, privy councillor in 1616, lord keeper in 1617, lord chancellor in 1618, Bacon verulum of Verulam in 1618 and finally Viscount St. Albans in 1621. His political pursuits, wealth, and influence evaporated when, only a few days after his last appointment, charges of bribery were brought against him. He was found guilty on his own confession, removed from all offices, imprisoned in the tower for a few days, and gradually stripped of all political pride and magnanimity. He died with debts amounting to well over twenty thousand pounds.

Throughout his political career Bacon was actively engaged in writing natural philosophy. Although in his later years he was deprived of lectureships at Cambridge and Oxford universities on this subject, his writings have hitherto aroused great interest and respect. In France, one of the earliest disciples of Bacon was Gassendi, who maintained that Bacon's "new and perfect method" was "a truly heroic enterprize."[1] And although cast in less praiseworthy terms,

Descartes also evaluated Bacon's literary pursuits rather highly. Above all, he observed that "it is only since the time of Bacon that the human mind has followed a proper plan in matters of philosophy."[2]

The designation of Bacon as a point of arrival and departure in modern natural philosophy has not been confined to writers of the first half of the seventeenth century. In 1669, Leibnitz referred to Bacon as a "divine genius."[3] At the turn of the eighteenth century an analogy was made between Bacon and Moses: both led the aimless and wandering out of darkness and into the "promised land."[4] Confidence in Bacon's formulas exemplified a kind of cumulative continuity. "Perhaps the greatest philosopher who ever lived was Lord Chancellor of England," declared Rousseau.[5] Bentham called him a "resplendent genius" and suggested the "true light" he shed on the arts and sciences will never be forgotten.[6] These acknowledgments of the influence of Bacon's philosophical efforts did not end with either Marx's consideration of him as one of the exponents of the new "materialistic mode of production" or with the nineteenth century as a whole.[7] The best example of this is John Dewey's assessment of Bacon as the "real founder of modern thought."[8]

Notwithstanding his supporters, Bacon has been severely reproached in modern history. His opposition has generally assumed a twofold character. On the one hand have been those who opposed the originality of his supposedly new contribution to philosophy. As one French critic expressed, "C'est Galilee, qui a montré l'art de l'interroger par l'experience. On a souvent attribué cette gloire à Bacon; mais ceux qui lui en font honneur, on été (à notre avis) un peu prodigues d'un bien qu'il ne leur appartenait peut-être pas de dispenser."[9] ("It was Galileo who examined the unknown by experiment. This glory has often been attributed to Bacon, but those who gave him this credit were [in our own opinion] a bit lavish with an honor that was perhaps not theirs to bestow.") Somewhat more mild was Sir John Herschel's belief that there was no real difference "between the doctrines which Bacon preached and those which Galileo practiced."[10]

The other half of the battle against Bacon has been waged by those concerned with the inconclusiveness of his scientific method. In this respect, we are reminded of Goethe's claim that "before one could achieve the simplification and conclusion by induction, even the kind

Bacon recommended, life would have gone and one's power would have been consumed."[11] Goethe's more extreme views, however, were untenable to Mill, who sought to reconcile the so-called tentative hypotheses of Bacon's inductive reasoning with a more general theory of induction. "Why is a single instance, in some cases," he says, "sufficient for a complete induction, while, in others, myriads of concurring instances without a single exception known or presumed, go such a very little way toward establishing a universal proposition? Whoever can answer this question knows more of the philosophy of logic than the wisest of the ancients and has solved the problem of induction."[12]

Alongside this matter of Bacon's inductive method may be added another criticism, which flows necessarily from an opposition to purely inductivist approaches to philosophical reasoning. The argument here is that Bacon's method of observing, analyzing, and recording *instantiae Naturae* crawled along gradually, step by step, and thus disregarded one crucial factor in scientific discovery: intuition or imagination. As one of Bacon's biographers put it, "In truth he was so afraid of assumptions and 'anticipations' and prejudices . . . that he missed the true place of the rational and formative element in his account of Induction."[13] Another commentator has drawn attention to those endeavors that seek general laws by digging tirelessly into minute facts. Unequivocal with "these Bacon-engendered philosophers," he concludes by asking whether "because the snail is sure of foot, for this reason must we clip the wings of the eagles?"[14]

These considerations of Bacon excite a kind of desire to know on what grounds they have been made, which, in turn, requires some careful reflection and analysis of Bacon's philosophical outlook. His principles and method of philosophizing have exercised a powerful and positive influence on modern thought, as well as being the subject of much adverse criticism. Bacon as a politician and Bacon the philosopher are doubtless subjects far too great to consider at the same time with any but crude results. One may be tempted then, to deal with these topics in themselves. But the plan of this chapter is even narrower in focus. I intend to point out the various ways that Bacon's philosophical program can be characterized as an undertaking in quantification. In a sense, this subject may be reduced ultimately to a type of dialogue comprising the procedures of scientific investigations and, the precision of mathematical conceptions. But the two sides of this dialogue lead to much the same conclusion although their routes may differ.

Peculiar Problems Connected with Bacon's Writings

Before we turn to the development of Bacon's philosophy and see how strong the element of what we may call quantification is in his reasonings, it is necessary to emphasize a few preliminary problems and draw some initial distinctions that any treatment of his program presupposes.

First, we are faced with the fundamental problem that many of Bacon's compositions remain incomplete. As Anderson remarks in his introduction to the *Novum Organum*, "The reader inherits much less than half of what Bacon for years hoped and intended to bequeath to future generations."[15] These unfinished works include several of his main earlier writings: *Temporis Partus Masculus* (c. 1603), *De Interpretatione Naturae Procemium* (1603), *Valerius Terminus of the Interpretation of Nature* (1603), *Cogitationes de Natura Rerum* (1604), *Cogiatationes de Scientia Humana* (1604), and his later major work, *Novum Organum* (1620), which was revised according to Rawley, no fewer than twelve times. At first sight, this incompleteness might appear to be a relatively major hurdle. Yet there remains a considerable amount of philosophical writings from which a fairly clear meaning of Bacon's ideas can be obtained. The matter becomes even less complicated when we find that Bacon's thought unfolded in a gradual, systematic manner. Many of the fundamental ideas treated in his early works reappear in later works with some slight modifications. Hence it is plausible to understand Bacon's philosophical framework removed from a chronological analysis. In the development of his thought, there was no great dividing line or turning point that may be said to have created an unusual, significant break in the sequence of his writings except, perhaps, career interruptions.

Second, because Bacon was primarily concerned with refuting the knowledge of antiquity and the all-embracing scholastic systems of philosophy, he never explicitly refers to any philosophical progenitors. Indeed he implores readers in his introductory paragraphs of the *Parasceve* (1620), to do "away with antiquities, and citations or testimonies of authors."[16] Hence any attempt to derive a prior philosophical line of descent for Bacon will prove fruitless. We can, of course, suggest certain works he was familiar with and others that he seems to have read closely.

As "every individual is a child of his time . . . it is just as absurd to fancy that a philosophy can transcend its contemporary world as it is to fancy that an individual can overleap his own age, jump over Rhodes."[17] And it is accurate to say, I think, that Bacon would not be disposed to reject this Hegelian point of view of grounding the philosopher's business in a strong dose of the actual, the present, rather than with what ought to be. To be sure, Bacon continuously insists that his philosophy was an offspring of time. In a Letter to James I, Bacon observes, "I am wont for my own part to regard this work as a child of time rather than of wit."[18]

Bacon thus took seriously the whole of world knowledge inasmuch as he possessed a particular understanding of it and insofar as he was acquainted with the experiments and conclusions drawn during his own lifetime. He stated his own position on this matter as early as 1592 in a letter to his uncle, the Lord Treasurer Burghley. "I confess," he says, that "I have taken all knowledge to be my province."[19]

This much we can be sure of: Bacon's intellectual landscape received some of its bearings from the unprecedented scientific revolution that occurred in the late Renaissance. Indeed Bacon implicitly accords primacy to three of the masterpieces that appeared then: Copernicus's *De Revolutionibus Orbium Coelestrium* (1543), Vesalius's *De Fabrica Hamani Corporis* (1543), and Cardano's *Artis Magnae Sive de Regulis Algebraicis* (1545). True, there are blemishes and a few major defects in some of Bacon's observations about phenomena. And there are some important omissions.

It is a matter of surprise, for example, that Bacon (as well as Descartes) did not know of, or perhaps ignored, Kepler's three laws of planetary motion.[20] He also seems to have overlooked John Napier's discovery of logarithms, which, through the use of ratios, enabled arithmetical and geometrical progressions to be reduced to simple relations. In the fifth book of his *De Augmentis Scientiarum* (1623), Bacon expounds the theoretical advancement demonstrated by Galileo around 1590 that falling bodies fall with equal velocities, keeping his tongue in his cheek insofar as credit to the latter is concerned.[21]

Thus when Bacon emphasizes that his basic task is to review the present state of human learning and to remove all of the former defects "that hath hindered the progression of learning," one is justified in calling into question the extent to which this vivid and certainly very impressive idea was in fact carried out.[22] If, however, one approaches Bacon from the standpoint that his enthusiastic ideas were never specifically realized, this runs the risk of overexpectation. Indeed, some have maintained that Bacon's *Advancement of Learning* was, paradoxically, no more than one of the "idle studies" he was attempting to replace. What this outlook misses, however, is the publicist side of Bacon's vocation, for as Bacon himself insists, "I only sound the clarion, but I enter not into battle." And elsewhere he says that philosophy must be built upon "the collecting and perfecting of a Natural and Experimental History . . . I have provided the machine, but the stuff must be gathered from the facts of nature."[23] We can also see the modesty in Bacon's judgment upon his own work in the introduction to *Natural and Experimental History* where he concludes, "The method which I have employed is explained, for there may be a mistake, and it may stimulate others to devise better and more exact methods."[24]

It is, then, as a corrective that we have suggested both Bacon's all-inclusive claims as well as his more tempered suggestions. His philosophical accounts can best be understood as a sort of halfway point between grandiose intentions and very limited conclusions. In Church's view, "Bacon was one of those men to whom posterity forgives a great deal, for the greatness of what he has done *and attempted* for posterity."[25]

The last point worth considering with reference to this general outlook of Bacon's works and various interpretations concerns the problem of style. Some of Bacon's philosophical and quasi-scientific treatises were the first to be published in the English language. English writers before him wrote in either Latin or Greek, and when their works were penned in English, they dealt with moral concerns rather than with scientific and philosophic developments. Hooker's and Baldwin's writings, for instance, fall within this former category.[26] Bacon himself was suspicious, to a certain extent, of the possible literary qualities the English language possessed.[27] It must also be remembered that, in the main, the movement that renounced the swelling, ornamental, and rhetorical style of the ancients did not begin until the

Royal Society commenced its stylistic reformation in the late 1600s although this was engineered earlier by Bacon.[28] We therefore should expect to find some words and expressions, especially in Bacon's *Of the Advancement of Learning*, that invariably functioned better at the time than now.

Bacon believed that the form of delivery was best carried out by aphorisms. He employed these short and somewhat pithy maxims in both books of *Novum Organum* and in the eighth book of *De Augmentis*. In using aphorisms, according to Bacon, "illustration and excursion are cut off; variety of examples is cut off; deduction and connexion are cut off; descriptions of practice are cut off; so there is nothing left to make the aphorisms of but some good quantity of observation."[29] Thus Bacon used a new and unusual linguistic style and also made the first attempt to realize a clear, plain, definite linguistic standard that sought to come as close to mathematical exactness as possible. "The first distemper of learning," says Bacon, is "when men study words and not matter [things]."[30]

The Division of Knowledge

Bacon's division of the sciences evidenced a rather marked architectonic character. The general outlines of this arrangement can be found in *Of the Advancement of Learning*; he reformulated a more detailed version in *De Augmentis*. According to Bacon, "knowledges are as pyramides," and from this line of thought emerged a set of interrelated sciences into a single, hierarchical flow of knowledge. At the base of Bacon's pyramid were the important natural or experimental histories. Writing and compiling a natural history was reminiscent of Pliny's *Natural History*, but, as Bacon emphasized, his natural history differed from the labors of the ancients insofar as it contained experiments of the mechanical arts rather than a simple classification of natural species.[31]

Bacon placed physics directly after natural history and immediately before the apex of knowledge, metaphysics. From the outset, Bacon proposed to show that the Aristotelian division of sciences was ill founded and essentially deadlocked. As Aristotle had maintained, the identification of a causal relation in a given subject should always stem from specific predicates of the phenomena alone. In other words, the principles and causes of physics, politics, and ethics, for example, are independent substances and should be treated differently from each other. An examination of the sources in Aristotle's *Physics*, for instance, concerns the subjects "Time," "Void," "Light," and "Heavy," whereas *Politics* refers strictly to elements within its own discipline: "Justice," "Kinship," and so on. It follows, according to peripatetic principles, that causal relations are best sought exclusively within the facts and propositions peculiar to a field of study.[32]

For Bacon, however, the cause of the existence of a thing is always best explained when it is viewed as a unified, undivided set of similar relations. Bacon therefore refused to separate the sciences in general; the methodology, or specific rules, whereby knowledge may be grasped; and the ultimate aim that the various forms of knowledge strived for.[33] In the first book of *Novum Organum*, he wrote that "the range of natural philosophy [must] take in the particular sciences, and the referring or *bringing back* of the peculiar sciences to natural philosophy; that the branches of knowledge may not be severed and cut off from the stem."[34] And again, "For when a philosophy is entire, it supports itself, and its doctrines give light and strength the one to the other; whereas if it be broken, it will seem strange and dissonant."[35]

In looking at the subdivisions of physics and metaphysics, Bacon spoke of the former as a type of inquiry principally concerned with determining "material and efficient causes." As he suggests, this involves analyzing the facts of nature in a horizontal manner, taking into consideration the amount and kinds of matter that are either united or diffused. The first part distinguishes the inviolable laws of nature, or first principles of things, which are necessary and forced upon us.[36] The subject matter of diffused physics concerns the whole realm of sense phenomena as manifestations or accidents that are not natural laws but that nevertheless can be ordered and described. By becoming acquainted with the many different kinds of substances in a given phenomenon, we may eventually come to know what Bacon calls "the sum of things." This is one of several places where Bacon invokes a quantity or serial order to understand the composition of a physical entity: "One method of delivery alone remains to us, which is simply this: we must lead men to the particulars themselves, and their series and order."[37]

Before turning to the makeup of Baconian metaphysics, it is worthwhile to draw attention to a significant feature in Bacon's account of physics, the so-called Appendice of Physics. This section was excluded in the early *The Advancement* and is first presented in the third book of *De Augmentis*. Here Bacon considers the measurements of motions and insists how important a recognition of this value is. How much motion found in a substance or body, Bacon tells us, constitutes the genuine part of investigations into physical phenomena.[38] Bacon also recognizes that studies that either ignore or take too lightly measuring of matter are open to potential superficiality and error. He warns us "that the calculating and ordination of the true degrees, moments, limits, and laws of motion and alterations (by means whereof all works and effects are produced), is a matter of far other nature than to consist in easy and wild generalities."[39] For Bacon, therefore, compiling observations of phenomena, understanding the status of the first principles of nature, and determining the quantity of increase and decrease of moving things are all part of his scheme of physics.

In contrast to physics, which deals with material and efficient causes, metaphysics, according to Bacon, treats formal and final causes. Bacon estimated that metaphysics lies beyond the substances studied in natural history and physics and is therefore properly placed at the vertical point of the pyramid of knowledge. As such, metaphysics constitutes a sort of summary philosophy or science of forms. Losee has rightly observed that "Bacon's Forms are neither Platonic forms nor Aristotelian formal causes."[40] Plato's forms, like those of Aristotle, were permanent and knowable because they were definitely enclosed and limited. They thus excluded matter as an intelligible form because it is illimitable and infinite; that is, it is susceptible to constant change. Plato, says Bacon, "lost the real fruit of his opinion by considering of forms as absolutely abstracted from matter, *and not confined and determined by matter.*"[41] Bacon's forms were not defined by their mean size or shape. Instead they represented a composite of relations that could be found in "every sort of matter." Thus "to inquire the form of a lion, of an oak, of gold, nay even of water and air, is a vain pursuit; but to inquire the form of dense, rare, hot, cold, heavy, light, tangible, pneumatic, volatile, fixed, and the like, as well as configurations of motions," is the true object of scientific inquiry.[42] It is these subordinate elements of the material things themselves that can be dissected and arranged into component parts—that is, conceived as an amount or quantity. Bacon's forms, then, are not qualitatively different entities; rather they are the "simple natures" of objects in respect to their increase and diminution.[43]

Bacon gives one form, heat, greater consideration than any other kind. In describing this form of motion, Bacon uses a set of "Tables of Instances" to discern observable properties of the form. The object of the first table is to identify present and nonpresent elements, asking if one attribute exists and another is absent. For example, effects that we find most displayed in flame, such as burning and melting, are likely to be absent in an inquiry into ice. This illustration is significant because it shows the inherent limitation in an inquiry of affirmative and negative properties, as well as the need for a further, more definite type of inquiry; as we well know, it is possible to speak of an intense coldness, say, from continuously holding an ice cube, as a burning sensation. For this reason, we must have recourse to another table, which Bacon calls the "Table of Degrees."

In the *Novum Organum* Bacon points out that in order to know fully the operative nature of a form (as opposed to an ill-defined or abstract one), "we must make a presentation to the understanding of instances in which the nature under inquiry is found in different degrees, more or less."[44] Only in this way can we rescue the "Table of Presence and Absence" from the dilemma of ultimate identification. Referring again to the example of the flame and ice cube, only by regarding these two objects from a quantitative point of view can we determine that the one is distinguished by a high degree of heat and the other by a very low degree.

The matter or nature of Bacon's forms is fixed such that a change in the motion of a form will lead correspondingly to a change in the form itself. It follows that the essence of heat is motion, which is already constituted as something given in itself. In fact, "no nature can be taken as the true form, unless it always decreases when the nature in question decreases, and in a like manner always increases when the nature in question increases."[45]

According to Bacon, it is indispensable to begin an inquiry with a collection of concrete facts, or data, which then must be classified and ordered into categories. This is the first stage of the study; it would be a mistake to restrict one's activities to this level. We next turn to the middle phase of physics. Here the inquiry seeks to ascertain the "variable or respective causes" of heat, such as the sun, friction from bodies rubbed together, volcanic activity, and so forth. Both natural history and physics, however, play a limited role in the investigation of objects. Finally, by searching into the simple natures of heat through metaphysics, we can obtain an accurate image of the form itself. From this can be drawn a definition, such as, "Heat is a motion, expansive, restrained, and acting in its strife upon the smaller particles of bodies."[46]

Method

Like Plato, Bacon may be said to have waged a particular and, at the same time, a universal crusade. For Plato, refuting the tenets of the sophists became a foremost preoccupation. But we may perceive in his teaching a more general conclusion, much more manifold in its scope, which he was attempting to put forward. Professor Barker has given the following assessment: "He was a gadfly who stung men into a sense of truth; he gave the shock of the torpedo-fish; he practiced the art of midwifery, and brought thought to birth. He appealed to what was in man's own mind, and trusted it to respond to the appeal."[47] Bacon too directed his remarks against a particular group; in his case, it was the peripatetic school of philosophy. He says in a well-known passage, "We copy the sin of our first parents while we suffer for it." But on a wider scale, Bacon was not just raising questions and criticizing the methods and principles of his predecessors; like Plato, he was trying to build a new foundation for learning.

Similar to Plato's belief, Bacon held as early as 1592 in his "Praise of Knowledge," "The mind is the man and knowledge the mind. A man is but what he knoweth."[48] But lurking behind this statement is an unrelenting doubt Bacon himself held regarding the mind's ability to seek knowledge independently, such as illustrated in Plato's dialogue with Meno's slave. To be sure, it was one of the original standards set forth by Bacon that the faculties of understanding must be "supplied with helps." This attitude is in marked contrast to Plato's endless faith in the mind's independent ability to gain an understanding of the phenomena in nature.[49]

From a purely historical point of view, the demand that the existing situation of knowledge be awakened from its slumber by a new and active method is a common thread that may be sewn among several thinkers besides Bacon. The emphatic concern with method at the turn of the seventeenth century was an observation that Pope, among others, singled out as a dominant characteristic of that period:

> Those Rules of old discovered, not devised,
> Are Nature still, but Nature methodised.[50]

Both Descartes and Hobbes, for instance, appealed explicitly to the efficacy of their own particular methods as the vehicles to infallible knowledge.[51]

It is not my purpose here to make any sharp distinctions between the different methods employed at this time by other thinkers and Bacon's own procedures. I can say, however, that for Bacon, the dependence on method was conclusive. Everything will be left hanging in the air (as were the meager and inept formulations of the scholastics) without it. A full appreciation of Bacon's overriding concern with the matter is evident from the following important statement from his preface to the second book of the *Novum Organum*, in which he says of his method:

Though hard to practice, is easy to explain; and it is this. I propose to establish progressive stages of certainty. The evidence of the sense, helped and guarded by a certain process of correction, I retain. But the mental operation which follows the act of sense I for the most part reject; and instead of it I open and lay out a new and certain path for the mind to proceed in, starting directly from the simple sensuous perception. The necessity of this was felt no doubt by those who attributed so much importance to Logic; showing thereby that they were in search of helps for the understanding, and had no confidence in the native and spontaneous process of the mind. But this remedy comes too late to do any good, when the mind is already, through the daily intercourse and conversation of life, occupied with unsound doctrines and beset on all sides by vain imaginations. And therefore that art of Logic, coming (as I said) too late to the rescue, and no way able to set matters right again, has had the effect of fixing errors rather than disclosing truth. There remains but one course for the recovery of a sound and healthy condition,—namely, that the entire work of the understanding be commenced afresh, and the mind itself be from the very outset not left to take its own course, but guided at every step; and the business be done as if by machinery.[52]

A detailed analysis of Bacon's method will reveal three stages that, taken together, form a systematic process of development. Whether his method may serve as a successful guide to understanding is another question. Furthermore, it is my intention to show in what respects Bacon's method may be said to be scientific.

The first stage exhibited in Bacon's method is grounded in the power of reduction; it starts with the presence of an object and then distinguishes its concrete and particular attributes. Bacon was convinced that the human intellect did not utilize its full potentiality, from "whence follows manifold ignorance of things."[53] But another aspect of this was his belief that knowledge may be "reduced to a better" and "less arbitrary and inconstant" condition.[54] To do this requires looking at the world with an eye to "reducing the non-sensible to the sensible."[55] By "sensible" Bacon means the corporeal world; finding the causes of sensible material as such had far better results than investigations into the divine universe. Accordingly, "You need [first] a reduction back to certainty."[56] This, however, is not enough. We are, asserts Bacon, concerned with obtaining knowledge wholly freed from doubt, especially the unreliable truths we impatiently grab from purely sensory knowledge. There have been, after all, too many abstract and "thorny" methods hitherto developed. "Therefore," says Bacon, "the reduction must be, that the bodies or parts of bodies so intermingled as before be of a certain grossness or magnitude; for the unequalities which move the sight must have a further dimension and quantity than those which operate many other effects."[57] We can conclude from this remark that the forms of corporeity must be reduced to the most definite measure possible.

The second stage of Bacon's methodology perhaps is best seen as interconnected with the first one and certainly inexplicable without it. In Bacon's view, knowledge that is "comprehended in exact methods . . . finds footing in due stages and degrees of certainty."[58] In the first case we were faced with identifying general and obscure things as exactly as possible, but an even clearer account is required. Mere reduction to immediate and simple entities is not enough. Hence, Bacon notes, it is necessary that knowledge also be founded on experimentation. "The best demonstration by far is experience."[59] And in this case the greater the number of experiments, the better will be the results of the research. One is reminded of the story of the peasant woman who fed her hen a double dose of grain in hope that it would return to her twice the normal number of eggs laid; but at length, the hen was overcome with so much food that it died. From this extract Bacon concludes, "It will not be safe to rely on any experiment in nature, unless it has been tried both in greater and lesser quantities."[60]

Attention has already been drawn to the special rules Bacon laid down as the groundwork to judgments made from experience: the detailed preparation of a natural history, arrangements of instances, and induction, "the very key to interpretation," which undertook a review of the instances from which a more general axiom could be established. Even these considerations along with the first stage, Bacon maintains, are inadequate. And here Bacon argues for the last feature of his claim, the use of scientific instruments.

Bacon's choice of these aids to learning representing the third stage of his method requires little comment. It should be noted, however, that for Bacon these instruments were not purely mechanical. When he referred to "instruments for understanding" he meant both physical and mental leanposts. The telescope, for example, could fit the character of the first class, whereas a well-founded theoretical method to guide practical studies could be taken for the reasoning category. As for the importance of this stage, Bacon spoke quite highly of it in the first book of the *Novum Organum*. Nevertheless the feeling prevails that this stage for Bacon was meant more to augment the previous arrangements than to culminate the path of scientific discovery.

Bacon's position in *De Augmentis* appears to support this interpretation. In the fifth book of this work he made an important point: although instruments are of some use, even these are not capable of producing knowledge of a thing's nature as it is.[61] Too often conclusions drawn from the use of scientific instruments are merely "appearances." Thus as Spedding points out concerning the skeptical reception Bacon gave to certain discoveries:

Now that nine years has passed since the discovery of Jupiter's satellites, the spots in the sun, etc., and no new discovery of importance had been announced, he wondered how it could be that men seeing so much further should be able to see no little more than they did, and began to suspect that it was owing to some defect either in the instrument or in the methods of observation.[62]

Turning from the character of Bacon's method to its application, we find again a decisive point of departure from the peripatetic tradition. According to Aristotle, there were basic divisions between each of the sciences, along with common properties to them all. Bacon, however, denied this proposition and held that one method alone could extend over all the fields of knowledge. "It may be asked," Bacon remarked, "whether I speak of natural philosophy only, or whether I mean that of the other sciences, logic, ethics, and politics, should be carried on by this method. Now I certainly mean what I said to be understood of them all."[63] Bacon's real point here is that the traditional segregation of the sources of knowledge was not necessarily or universally valid. Moreover, by mixing the particular sciences with the study of philosophy, the ultimate business at hand, demonstrative knowledge, would be accelerated.

In emphasizing science as the so-called mother of power in Bacon's philosophical writings, I have overlooked one very important feature.[64] This is the subject of mathematics, and its place in Bacon's philosophy stands in great need of explanation. In Bacon's words, "Inquiries into nature have the best result, when they begin with physics and end in mathematics."[65]

The Importance of Mathematics

It remains for us to ask what Bacon's position was with respect to the branch of mathematics. Did he share an interest in the mathematical literature and methods prominent in his time? Did his approach to experimental philosophy admit of a preoccupation with mathematics? Is there any currency to the claim that the focus of his analysis was quantitative rather than qualitative in character?

Of the numerous commentators who have assessed Bacon's works, the most common observation to be found is that Bacon himself was not a mathematician.[66] From this an initial conclusion is usually drawn to the effect that this factor impeded his evaluation of things mathematically.[67] Another argument put forward ignores Bacon's personal circumstances but maintains that his philosophical inquiry widely missed the mark of the scientific movement characteristic of the seventeenth century. It is suggested that Bacon's qualitative observations are thus unrepresentative of other philosophical undertakings flourishing in a tentatively scientific and quantitative milieu. Professor Whitehead has expressed this view:

Bacon completely missed the tonality which lay behind the success of seven-teenth-century science. Science was becoming and has remained, primarily quantitative. Search for measurable elements among your phenomena, and then search for relations between these measures of physical quantities. Bacon ignores this rule of science . . . he gives no hint that there should be a search for quantities.[68]

According to a commonly held view, then, Bacon's approach to philosophy lends itself better to a treatment in terms of quality than a quantitative perspective.[69] This thesis adheres to the standpoint that Bacon was ignorant in quantifiable problems and that his studies were not the result of an application of mathematical formulas and procedures.

Although Bacon was not extremely well versed in the study of mathematics, this does not mean he was unaware of the value of its propositions. Nor does it follow that Bacon was opposed to mathe-matical cognition. Indeed we find in Bacon's own testimony that the accusation alleging he was unknowing of the pioneering work done in mathematics is unsupportable. In several places, he refers to Giro-lamo Cardano, whose *Artis Magnae Sive de Regulis Algebraicis* (1545) was considered a breakthrough in the field of mathematics.[70] There is, however, no evidence as to how conversant Bacon was in arithmetic and algebra.

In order to understand the particular interest Bacon had in mathe-matics, we must turn to the relevant passages in his philosophical works. As we have seen, Bacon was preoccupied with rendering the pursuit of knowledge as absolute and infallible as possible. The ac-tivity of the mind, according to Bacon, "is strangely eager to be relieved from suspense, and to have something fixed and immov-able."[71] What will not provide this security for the mental processes is clear enough for Bacon: the anticipations and discoveries of tradi-tional thought, an inductive method that disregards negative or contradictory instances, and any simple testimony of the sensations.

Through mathematics, combined with physics, the mind may begin to approach what Bacon considers undisputed and unprejudiced knowledge. As he explains in the second book of *Novum Organum*, "Inquiries into nature have the best result when they begin with phys-ics and end in mathematics . . . the business [here] being transferred from the complicated to the simple; *from the incommensurable to the commensurable; from surds to rational quantities; from the infinite and vague to the finite and certain.*"[72] In other words, the real nature of a phenomenon is brought to light when it ends in mathematics in the sense of demonstration. This is so only if there have been preceding quantifications requiring calibrated instruments, techniques of application, display of results in tables, and the formulation of equations and propositions embodying rules of measure.

Thus Bacon hardly neglected the place of mathematics in philosophical investigations. In fact, mathematical reasoning displayed a striking degree of certainty and aid to comprehension. We can see exactly how influential it was in a statement Pope made toward the end of the seventeenth century. His analysis of the growth of the sciences concluded, "Mad Mathesis alone was unconfined" and triumphed over the other sciences.[73]

In a more detailed consideration of the progress of the scientific movement, Bacon, decades prior to Pope's sketch, had come to the same conclusion.[74] Because of the certainty of its concepts and procedures, mathematics had developed to the point of exercising dominion over the natural sciences.

It will be recalled from the earlier discussion of Bacon's division of knowledge into three branches that mathematics was one particular science that was omitted, but this is not entirely correct. True, mathematics was not primary to Bacon's pyramid of knowledge; he did not consider it an independent branch of study as Aristotle esteemed it to be. Instead he treated mathematics as an appendix and auxiliary science to all other sciences.

The reason why Bacon exalted the characteristic features of mathematics yet assigned it a status of less importance than either physics or metaphysics is not as clear as some others have maintained. At first glance, it seems that Bacon was reacting against the Pythagorean faith in number as being applicable to contemplative matter that had no material substance by relegating mathematics to a position inferior to physics (the study of active matter). One might certainly expect this from a man who held the school of Democritus in higher esteem than that of Plato or Aristotle. Nevertheless, his assertion that research is best employed if it begins with physics and ends in mathematics suggests that progress in mechanics is useless without mathematical computations.

In this sense, Bacon may be understood as assigning a very high-level position to mathematics in seeking solutions and principles to the causes of things. Bacon is probably best seen in the light of this latter characterization of clearly advocating that an important place be given to mathematical formulations. It must be noted, Bacon wrote, "that everything relating both to bodies and virtues in nature be set forth (as far as may be) numbered, weighed, measured, defined . . . and when exact proportions cannot be obtained, then we must have recourse to indefinite estimates and comparatives."[75] Furthermore, Bacon held that quantitative differentiation in the investigation into the composition or nature of a thing was not enough. The determinations produced from these initial observations belong to the "informative part" of each subject matter. The real focus of interest is the total matter or final product, which is exclusively a concern of the "operative part" of an investigation. As he put it:

The chief cause of failure in operation (especially after natures have been diligently investigated) is the ill determination and measurement of the forces and actions of bodies. Now the forces and actions of bodies are circumscribed and measured, either by distances of space, or by moments of time, or by concentration of quantity, or by predominance of virtue; and unless these four things have been well and carefully weighed, we shall have sciences, fair perhaps in theory, but in practice inefficient.[76]

Let us consider briefly an analysis composed along Baconian lines that comprises some quantified procedures. Suppose we wish to envisage the whiteness of an object. We are convinced of the whiteness we see in snow, marble, or paint, for example, but to free these substances from all of their properties except whiteness, we must reduce them to parts, unequal of course, but with a certain grossness or magnitude. "For the unequalities which move the sight must have a further dimension and quantity than those which operate many other effects."[77] Thus, to comprehend the abstraction called whiteness we must, according to Baconian principles, inquire into the division before the composition of an object by breaking it down into simple particulars.[78] We then move further to obtain a more exact conception of whiteness by measuring the degree of our perception of its being white and the degree to which our perceptual experience of other colors may be said to be missing. This method of breaking down or dissecting leads to an eventual empirical truth that Bacon refers to as a "definite point."[79] Our conception of whiteness will thus be the result of a number of observed distinctions and measurements. Degrees of our perceptual experience are to be calibrated and the absence of other colors measured.

An important consequence follows from this exercise. If we wish to interpret a given set of occurrences or phenomena in the world by means of Bacon's procedures, we are compelled to construct the range of possible experiences in terms of what is verifiable. And unless our investigations into the particular nature of things or, as Bacon refers to them, "Perogative Instances," can be measured and fixed accordingly, we cannot claim to have provided an exhaustive or accurate inquiry.[80] This principle, however, was bound to lead to the fundamental fallacy that all instances contain the potential of being provable or unprovable or determined according to a measurable ratio or degree.

The question now arises, if there is a markedly mathematical element in Bacon's analyses, how relevant is the factor of measure? And because measurement is not a condition itself, what criteria does he conceive by which things can be measured?

There were two things Bacon was doubtless obsessed with: aphorisms and dividing or defining subjects. He maintained that the former was the most appropriate way to express knowledge and the latter the best procedure whereby the phenomena of nature may be interpreted. After composing the *Novum Organum*, Bacon delineated in the *Parasceve* 130 particular histories of natural phenomena. And in the proceeding work, *De Augmentis*, he began by listing nearly 40 subdivisions of the arts and sciences. Students of Bacon are wont to claim that his exhaustive definitions hindered any substantial conceptions that he might have formulated. This is also the position we start from in examining the matter of what is to be measured and how it is to be carried out. It is not until Bacon is a third of the way through *De Augmentis* that he begins to consider the notion of measure. Generally his concern here is with mensuration in the context of political problems. Specifically, however, Bacon is concerned with three political duties confronting all forms of government: preservation, happiness and prosperity, and extension of empire. Taken together, these factors determine the "true greatness" of political associations.

What is especially peculiar to the affairs of civil government is that they "fall under measure" and are thus subject to "overmeasuring" or "undervaluing." It is therefore of critical importance that leaders of estates and kingdoms get their sums right by basing their judgments on rational calculation. In the past, the greatness and prosperity of kingdoms was left to mere chance, says Bacon. The need to end the disruptive accidents of political life was the need for correct calculations.

Bacon's suggestions for determining the quantitative relations of civil government run along the following lines. The power and forces of an empire must be measured according to proportions; number alone is insufficient to determine the strength and security of a nation, especially if its people are weak in courage. A wolf, Bacon points out, is never troubled by the apparent number of sheep.

Bacon stresses that the disposition of the people must be continuously warlike. The criterion for and the guide to a great kingdom could be found nowhere other than in the "honor," "study," and "occupation" of armaments and war. Only with the recognition of Bacon's unconditional adherence to war activities does it become possible to comprehend his claim that

no body can be healthful without exercise, neither natural body nor politic; and certainly, to a kingdom or estate, a just and honorable war is the true exercise. A civil war, indeed, is like the heat of a fever, but a foreign war is like the heat of exercise, and serveth to keep the body in health; for in slothful peace, both courages will effeminate and manners corrupt.[81]

In addition, it is also important to limit the population of nobility and, at the same time, to increase the number of naturalized subjects.

Bacon seems to be contending two points here and in his essay, "Of the True Greatness of Kingdoms and Estates." First, civil government is conducive to a standard of measure and computation.[82] Only this approach to the problems of justice and administration will establish a rational and proportionate political system. Second, this standard must be based on a degree of distributive equality whereby the members of the state—in Bacon's case, the noblemen, gentlemen, yeomanry, and military—are not inferior to each other.[83]

Bacon's representation of a symbolic form of distributive justice was based on the analogy between mathematics and justice. This is to be found, according to Bacon, in the rule that says, "Things that are equal to the same are equal to each other."[84] The analogy, however, is not merely coincidental to standards of distribution. The view is everywhere present in the character of civil government. As Bacon says of Machiavelli, the great principle he laid down was that states are best governed when reduced, *ad principia*, a conclusion gained from both mathematics and physics.[85]

As far as concerns Bacon's remarks about mathematics, then, it is difficult to claim that the bulk of his ideas were couched in mathematical thinking. However, critics of Bacon who maintain that mathematics did not affect the direction of his philosophical discourses barely scratch the surface of his formulations. For Bacon, the efficacy and testimony of applied mathematical reasoning was of crucial importance in demonstrating the certainty of propositions in "experimental philosophy." His belief that the shortcoming of all previous studies was due to the fact that they were neither "verified," "counted," "weighed," nor "measured" led him to overemphasize these attributes in his own philosophy.[86] Unquestionably it may be said that Bacon's preoccupation with quantitative determinations was formulated out of deference to the mathematical field of inquiry rather than because of any technical skill as such.

According to Bacon, the best form of research is carried out in a like manner to the activity of the bee. It is no surprise that he chose this example from nature. The bee, working as it does with the utmost diligence and patience, constructs its cell according to absolute mathematical precision by which it can best attain the greatest degree of space within a very restricted structure. Just as the bee learns to apply mathematics to things in nature, so Bacon considered it fundamental to the equipment of natural philosophy.

The Operation of Quantity

Bacon, in assigning "Quantity" to the twenty-third Perogative Instance in the *Novum Organum*, noted that he borrowed the term from the field of medicine.[87] It was not until the last half of the sixteenth century that the modern spirit of observational research was introduced into medicine by Vesalius. Indeed Vesalius was the first to concentrate on the dissection of human beings strictly for research purposes. In so doing, he helped to alter continental philosophy in the sense that understanding human knowledge was no longer looked upon as an analysis involving the structural unity of the whole being; rather it examined separate problems that could be dissolved and dissected, and correlative solutions then could be found for the individual parts. To be sure, the study of medicine had a very positive effect on considerations of essences or forms in terms of quantifiable parts and bodies. Further, it does not seem particularly strange that Harvey, Hobbes, Coiter, and Fabricus were all acquainted with this development in the field of medicine, an event as important as the leap taken by Galen when he first dissected various kinds of animals.[88]

This is associated with the way Bacon grasped the particular meaning and function of quantity. In *De Augmentis*, for instance, he boldly asserted in Pythagorean terminology that quantity "is as it were the dose of Nature."[89] But Bacon's emphasis was later placed in more concrete terms than the view expressed by the Pythagorean tradition. In particular, the "dose" he referred to means a "quantity of body." And it is with this distinction that one must consider Bacon's endeavor to explain phenomena quantitatively—that is, as clusters of unspecific material bodies understood by reductive analyses and questions of how much. Above all, it must be recognized

that to calculate the proportions and quantities of matter existing in different bodies, and to find out by what industry and sagacity true information thereof may be procurred, is a very difficult thing. . . . Seeing therefore that it is a thing of all others the most fundamental and universal, we must gird ourselves up to deal with it; for indeed without it all philosophy is utterly . . . disorderly.[90]

It seems plausible to illustrate Bacon's conception of quantity from two points of view: first, as concerned with a rational specific reality far removed from speculative or conceptual interpretations, and second, as the key element in investigating and laying bare the content and nature of motion. If we look at the first viewpoint, it must be noted that Bacon held that quantity belonged within the confines of parameters, that is, as "determined" and "proportionable."[91] A physical property was thus conceived as something that could be measured or defined in terms of minima and maxima. Bacon remarked that a proper representation of a thing will pay equal attention to calculating elements on both sides of the scale. Disregarding the smallest amount of body or merely stressing the greatest quantity is therefore misleading, for no body, in Bacon's theory, contains "infinite being." Accordingly, "the quantity of matter, and how it is distributed in bodies, (abundantly in some, sparingly in others), no careful and methodical inquiry according to true or approximate calculations has been instituted."[92]

Bacon's aim, then, was meant to be more sophisticated than a simple count of physical characteristics in a given substance. It was meant to be more than an arithmetic process. His real interest was to determine and compute the relationships between and within bodies. Characterizing the properties of substances in terms of how much and how little was but the first procedure. Determining the proportion and magnitude of the properties themselves was his main goal.

Whatever concrete experiment Bacon transmitted to posterity from his quantitative thinking remains an entirely different issue from the suggestions he put forward. In the whole of Bacon's works, for instance, the only completed example we have of an experiment involving quantified determinations is his *History of Dense and Rare*. Here Bacon was concerned with the contraction and expansion of matter in space, and he provided a table showing the amount of space occupied by various given quantities. The table was, in fact, a revised version of his earlier work, *Phenomena of the Universe* (c. 1608). Yet, as he disclosed, there was considerable room for further investigation into measurements of this type, which may yield more exact results.[93]

Closely related to Bacon's conception of quantity as a body involving a definite and ascertainable amount of matter is the idea that motion lies at the root of a body's change or mutation: "It is quite certain that a body is affected only by a body; and that there is no local motion which is not excited by the parts of the body moved, or by the adjacent bodies."[94]

This second aspect of Bacon's view of quantity—how motion may be measured—is of central importance to philosophers, for "one who philosophises rightly, and in order, should dissect nature and not abstract her . . . and must by all means consider first matter as united to the first form, and likewise to the first principle of motion, as it is found."[95]

Measuring motion, says Bacon, is taking account of its dose of virtue: its length, speed, and degree of dependency upon another stimulus. All of the various virtues, however, remain augmented or diminished according to features common to all types of motion found in bodies. As such, the value attributed to one is precisely the value attributed to all other entities. In contradistinction to mere value, then, a predominance of virtue is simply an immanence or high concentration of quantity.

It seems an inescapable conclusion that mathematization was a very important feature of Bacon's philosophy. Critics may be right in saying that Bacon provided few solutions to the problems and methodological prerequisites he conceived, but they are wrong in recognizing him as a qualitative philosopher. In truth, Bacon insisted on quantitative conceptions to provide a new and striking example for the development of further theoretical and practical analyses.

Notes

1. Petrus Gassendi, *Opus Omnia* (Leyden, 1658), vol. 1, p. 62.
2. Descartes, *Discours de la Method* (Paris, 1724), pp. 128–29.
3. Leibnitz, *Oeuvres* (Paris, 1859–1875), vol. 4, p. 105.
4. Cowley, *Works*, 9th ed. (London, 1700), p. 40.
5. Rousseau, *Oeuvres* (Paris, 1959–1964), vol. 1.
6. Bentham, *Works* (Edinburgh, 1838–1843), vol. 8, p. 99.
7. Cf. Benjamin Farrington, *Francis Bacon: Philosopher of Industrial Science* (London, 1951), pp. 174–75.
8. John Dewey, *Reconstruction of Philosophy* (New York, 1950), p. 46.
9. M. Biot, *Biographie universelle*, vol. 16, p. 329, quoted in Macvey Napier, *Remarks Illustrative of the Scope and Influence of the Philosophical Writings of Lord Bacon* (Edinburgh, 1818), p. 2. See also a similar statement made over a century earlier in A. Baillet, *La vie de Monsieur Des-Cartes* (Paris, 1691), pp. 148–49.
10. See Bacon, *Works*, ed. James Spedding, Robert Ellis, and Douglas Heath (London, 1858), vol. 1, 3, p. 373 (hereafter referred to as *Works*).
11. Goethe, "Zur Farbenlehre," *Naturwiss*, vol. 3, p. 236, quoted in Ernst Cassier, *The Problem of Knowledge* (New Haven, Conn., 1950), p. 146.
12. John Stuart Mill, *System of Logic*, 8th ed. (London, 1889), p. 206.
13. R. W. Church, *Bacon*, English Men of Letters Series (London, 1884), p. 193. T. H. Huxley writes, "Those who refuse to go beyond fact rarely get as far as fact . . . almost every great step has been made by the 'anticipation of nature,' that is, by the invention of hypotheses which, though verifiable, often

had very little foundation to start with." Quoted in F. S. C. Northrop, *The Logic of the Sciences and the Humanities* (New York, 1947), pp. 10–11.

14. Edgar Allan Poe, "Eureka," in *The Science Fiction of Edgar Allan Poe*, ed. Harold Beaver (Middlesex, 1976), pp. 214, 216.

15. Francis Bacon, *The New Organon*, ed. Fulton H. Anderson (Indianapolis, 1960), p. xxxviii.

16. Bacon, *Philosophical Works*, ed. J. M. Robertson (London, 1905), p. 403 (hereafter referred to as *PW*).

17. Hegel, *Philosophy of Right*, trans. T. M. Knox, (Oxford, 1952), p. 11.

18. Bacon, *PW*, pp. 242, 279.

19. Bacon, "Letters and Life," *Works*, vol. 1, p. 109.

20. The first two laws were published in 1609 and the third law in 1619. See W. W. Rouse Ball, "European Science in the Seventeenth and Earlier Years of the Eighteenth Centuries," in *The Cambridge Modern History* (Cambridge, 1908), vol. 5, chap. 23.

21. Bacon, *PW*, p. 506. See also Spedding's statements in Bacon, *Works*, vol. 3, pp. 511ff, 725.

22. Bacon, *PW*, p. 76.

23. Bacon, *Works*, vol. 4, p. 12.

24. Ibid., vol. 5, p. 136.

25. Church, *Bacon*, p. 177. Emphasis added.

26. Cf. W. R. Sorley, *A History of English Philosophy* (Cambridge, 1920), p. 14.

27. See Bacon, "Letters and Life," *Works*, vol. 3, p. 429.

28. See the excellent studies by Richard Foster Jones in *The Seventeenth Century* (London, 1951).

29. Bacon, *PW*, p. 531.

30. Ibid., p. 54. See also Robert Boyle, *Philosophical Works*, ed. T. Birch (London, 1725), vol. 1, pp. 11, 29, 105.

31. See Bacon, *PW*, p. 289 (aphorism 98). Bacon's judgment is not altogether correct in this instance. See, for example, book 7 of Pliny's *Natural History*, trans. H. Rackham (London, 1838), vol. 1, which covers such subjects as philosophy, painting, sculpture, medicine, geometry, and architecture.

32. See Aristotle, *Metaphysics*, 980a23, 994b32–995a; *Ethics*, 1094b23. In *The Works of Aristotle*, ed. W. D. Ross (Oxford, 1925).

33. See Bacon, *PW*, p. 299 (aphorism 127) for his proposal to apply his method to all other sciences, including logic, ethics, and politics. Bacon's *telos*, or the ultimate purpose he conceived for philosophic inquiry, is a subject that has received extensive treatment elsewhere. See ibid., pp. 186, 194, 280, 286, 453; M. T. McClure, "Francis Bacon and the Modern Spirit,"

Journal of Philosophy 16 (1917): 502–27; Howard B. White, *Peace among the Willows* (The Hague, 1968).

34. Bacon, *PW*, p. 291 (aphorism 107). Emphasis added.

35. Ibid., p. 468.

36. Homer: "Much against your own will, since necessity lies more mightily upon you."

37. Bacon, *PW*, p. 263 (aphorism 36).

38. Ibid., p. 467.

39. Ibid., p. 200.

40. John Losee, *A Historical Introduction to the Philosophy of Science* (Oxford, 1972), p. 66.

41. Bacon, *PW*, pp. 94, 469. Emphasis added.

42. Ibid., p. 469.

43. Cf. Meyrick H. Carré, *Phases of Thought in England* (Oxford, 1949), p. 244.

44. Ibid., p. 315 (aphorism 13).

45. Ibid., p. 315.

46. Ibid., p. 326 (aphorism 20).

47. Sir Ernst Barker, *The Political Thought of Plato and Aristotle* (New York, 1959), p. 64.

48. Bacon, *Works*, vol. 8, p. 123, and Harl, MSS 6769, fo. 47.

49. See also the well-known account of Plato blaming his colleagues for using mechanical instruments in reducing the duplication of a cube: "The good of geometry is thereby lost and destroyed." Plato, *The Republic*, ed. F. Cornford (Oxford, 1941), p. 237.

50. *An Essay on Criticism* in *The Poetry of Pope*, ed. M. H. Abrams (New York, 1954), p. 11. See also Basil Wiley, *The Seventeenth Century Background* (Middlesex, 1934), chap. 2, and S. L. Bethell, *The Cultural Revolution of the Seventeenth Century* (London, 1951).

51. In *Rules for the Direction of the Mind*, Descartes explained, "By method I mean certain and single rules, such that by exact observation, he shall never assume what is false as true, and will never spend his mental efforts to no purpose, but will always gradually increase his knowledge and so arrive at a true understanding." *Philosophical Works*, trans. Elizabeth Haldane and G. R. T. Ross (Cambridge, 1911), vol. 1, p. 9. Hobbes, too, in the beginning of *De Corpore*, contended that "where there is need of a long series of reasons, there most men wander out of the way, and fall into error for want of method." *English Works*, ed. W. Molesworth (London, 1839), vol. 1, p. 1.

52. Bacon, *PW*, p. 256.

53. Bacon, *Works*, vol. 4, p. 4. Similar views have emerged in the nine-

teenth and twentieth centuries, particularly in the field of psychology.

54. Ibid.

55. Bacon, *PW*, p. 352 (aphorism 40).

56. Ibid., p. 197.

57. Ibid.

58. Ibid., pp. 59, 323 (aphorism 19).

59. Ibid., p. 274 (aphorism 70).

60. Ibid., p. 506.

61. Ibid., p. 504.

62. Ibid., p. 352 n. 87.

63. Ibid., pp. 299 (aphorism 127), 280 (aphorism 80).

64. This term is taken from White, *Peace among the Willows*, p. 99.

65. Bacon, *PW*, p. 307 (aphorism 8).

66. See, for example, Church, *Bacon*, p. 195, and the essay on Bacon in *The Encyclopedia Brittanica*, 11th ed., vol. 3, pp. 144–51.

67. See, for example, Losee, *Historical Introduction*, p. 67.

68. Alfred North Whitehead, *Science and the Modern World* (Glasgow, 1975), p. 61. See also Joseph J. Spengler, "On the Progress of Quantification in Economics," in *Quantification: A History of the Meaning of Measurement in the Natural and Social Sciences*, ed. Harry Woolf (New York, 1961), p. 133.

69. The following texts consider Bacon from a qualitative vantage point: Ralph Blake, Curt Ducasse, and Edward Madden, *Theories of Scientific Method: The Renaissance through the Nineteenth Century* (Seattle, 1960), p. 63; Carré, *Phases of Thought*, p. 245; Wiley, *Seventeenth Century Background*, chap. 2.

70. See Bacon, *Works*, vol. 3, pp. 530, 571, 603, and Leslie Ellis's preface to *Sylva Sylvarium* in ibid., pp. 326–27. Nowhere, however, does Bacon refer to other significant contributors in mathematics except Galileo. This includes such notables in England as Recorde, Billingsley, and Digges, as well as men on the Continent such as Tartaglia, Benedetti, Cataneo, Veglia, Stevin, and Vieta. But see Bacon's proposed history of mathematics in ibid., vol. 4, p. 270.

71. Bacon, *PW*, p. 515.

72. Ibid., p. 307 (aphorism 8). Emphasis added. The business engaged in where a mathematician is at work does not get transferred from the incommensurable to the commensurable. Bacon ought rather to have said that a mathematician throughout is concerned with both in relation of one to the other.

73. Cf. Louis I. Bredvold, *The Brave New World of the Enlightenment* (Ann Arbor, 1961), p. 38.

74. See Bacon, *PW*, p. 279 (aphorism 80).

75. Ibid., p. 406.

76. Ibid., pp. 359 (aphorism 44), 702.

77. Ibid., p. 197.

78. Ibid., p. 199.

79. Ibid., p. 202.

80. Bacon enumerates twenty-seven kinds of instances. Of these, the last seven pertain specifically to quantitative considerations. See ibid., pp. 359–86 (aphorisms 44–51).

81. Ibid., p. 773.

82. Compare the following account given by Hegel. The same doctrine, he says, may be applied to "politics, when the constitution of a state has to be looked at as independent of, no less than dependent on, the extent of its territory, the number of its inhabitants, and other quantitative points of the same kind." Hegel's *Logic*, trans. William Wallace, 3d. ed. (Oxford, 1975), sec. 108.

83. See Bacon, *PW*, p. 609.

84. See ibid., pp. 90–91.

85. Ibid., p. 91.

86. See ibid., p. 289 (aphorism 98).

87. Ibid., p. 365 (aphorism 47).

88. See C. Singer and C. Rabin, *A Prelude to Modern Science* (Cambridge, 1946), intro.

89. Bacon, *PW*, p. 476.

90. Bacon, *Works*, vol. 5, p. 339.

91. See Bacon, *PW*, p. 97.

92. Bacon, *Works*, vol. 5, p. 340. See also Bacon, *PW*, p. 339 (aphorism 34).

93. Bacon, *Works*, vol. 5, pp. 341–44.

94. Ibid., vol. 4, p. 202.

95. Bacon, *PW*, pp. 467, 651.

3

Quantitative Thinking in Hobbes

> There exists no certitude
> where some branch of the
> mathematical sciences cannot
> be applied.
>
> —*da Vinci*

When Thomas Hobbes of Malmesbury (1588–1679) left New College at Oxford, he became a page to the lord chancellor, Francis Bacon. The only information available regarding this event is to be found in Aubrey's *Brief Lives*, and even here, scant attention is paid to the matter. Aubrey, a close friend to Hobbes, remarks that Bacon "loved to converse" with Hobbes, who "assisted his lordship in translating severall of his Essayes into Latin, one, I well remember, is that *Of the Greatness of Cities*: the rest I have forgott."[1] More importantly, however, is the statement that follows to the effect that Bacon dictated his thoughts to Hobbes "because he understood what he wrote" unlike any of the predecessors to the secretariat post.[2] These clues hardly suggest any consistent link between these two eminent seventeenth-century thinkers. Indeed it is practically impossible to find Bacon mentioned in Hobbes's writings. In his completed works, Bacon is only referred to twice; once he is quoted in "An Answer to Bishop Bromhall" and the other time in confirmation of an experiment he carried out regarding the motions of water and air.[3] In view of the fact that among practically all leading writers subsequent to Bacon he is acknowledged as the founder of modern philosophy, it is noteworthy that Hobbes unhesitatingly disqualifies himself from this indebtedness.[4] The past, however, is generally an uncompromising restraint, and thus it would be well to examine some of the resemblances between the principles of Hobbes's philosophizing and that of Bacon's before setting out to chart their routes of divergence. To some extent, their endeavor may be conceived as an elaboration or continuum of the rational development of modern political philosophy.

This idea of conflating Bacon and Hobbes into one uniform network is not shared by many political historiographers, especially Brandt in his *Hobbes' Mechanical Conception of Nature*.[5] In it he makes the obvious seem absolute: whereas Bacon's method was inductive, Hobbes's approach to problems was deductive and thus "not at all Baconian."[6] This is a very seductive distinction that has been championed too fanatically by Hobbesian scholars. To this tradition of opposing inductive and deductive modes of reasoning, Professor Whitehead has aptly remarked, "It would be just as simple for the two ends of a worm to quarrel."[7] From this point of view, induction and deduction belong together, and it is misleading to view them as separate branches of logic. Investigations into heredity, for example, afford the most obvious relation between induction and deduction. In classifying particular or singular characteristics of an organism, we deduce, in turn, another organism by its specific hereditary features. It should also be noted that Bacon's method, or more precisely, his method of elimination (*Major est via instantae negativae*, as he called it), was not completely without an occasional appeal to higher laws of generality.[8]

Brandt also suggests a limited selection of features that may be considered common points—for instance, Bacon's conception of the act of sound, which can be found in his *Sylva Sylarium*. Brandt contends this is a "feasible comparison" to Hobbes, but it is purely "negligible." Finally, he recomposes his earlier position and gives a brief account of the "conception of spirit," which remains a common point of usage between Bacon and Hobbes. This is a valid contribution, however narrow-minded it may seem. In fact, it can be emphasized that Hobbes echoes Bacon on this matter. Bacon postulated that "air and spirit, and like bodies, which in their entire substance are rare and subtle, can neither be seen nor touched."[9] And among Hobbes's considerations of the general properties of physics, we find the following statement: "Spirit is thin, fluid, transparent, invisible body. The word in Latin signifies breath, air, wind and the like."[10]

But the disposition to liken Hobbes to Bacon has nevertheless found adherents. Among them is M. Sorbriére, who had correspondence with Hobbes and once wrote, "I scarce know two men in the world that have more different colours of speech than these two great wits."[11] Another Frenchman, Gaston Sortais, emphasized that Hobbes and Bacon were both utilitarians but that the difference between them consists primarily in their methodologies or the particularity of their styles. As he puts it, "Bref, Bacon pense surtout par métaphores et compose en poète. . . . Bref, Hobbes pense surtout par concepts et compose en géométre."[12] ("Briefly, Bacon thinks above all in metaphors and composes in poetry. . . . Hobbes thinks above all in concepts and composes in geometry.")

Still these accounts are no more than elementary observations, and to a certain extent, they fail to discern the compound conceptual similarities, as well as the variances between Bacon and Hobbes. One subject in particular deserves detailed attention here insofar as an evaluation of the influence Bacon had on Hobbes and the deviations of the latter from the former are concerned; this involves the so-called legitimate rules and end of philosophical inquiry.

It was in the nature of seventeenth-century thought to redeem philosophy from the speculative entanglements of previous ages. This nouveau philosophy, to which Platonic idealism and scholastic dogmatism were anathema, possessed an innermost adherence to empirical research and the objectivity projected by natural science.[13] Bacon and Hobbes were forerunners of this claim to immunize the object of philosophical investigations from the sentiments and corruption of the ancients. Their mode of procedure was to enunciate clearly the "true end of Philosophy" and then to classify the respective disciplines or subjects of philosophy. Regarding the first condition, Bacon set forth that the end of philosophy ought to be "to preserve and augment whatsoever is solid and fruitful," which means, as he disclosed in *Of the Advancement of Learning*, to make " 'Inquiry of Causes and Productions of Effects' so that man's livelihood may be 'better endowed.' "[14] According to Hobbes, who closely reflects Bacon in this realization, "The *end* or *scope* of philosophy is, that we may make use to our benefit of effects formerly seen; or that, by application of bodies to one another, we may produce the like effects of those we conceive in our mind, as far as matter, strength and industry, will permit, for the commodity of human life."[15] And similarly to Bacon, he asserts the well-known aphorism: "The end of knowledge is power."[16]

From the division of all human learning according to what he conceived as the three faculties of understanding—memory, imagination, and reason—Bacon formulated the individual object of philosophy, which corresponds to the third and most important faculty of the mind: *ratio*, or reasoning. History is conceived through memory and poesy through imagination. Under philosophy he included the "arts and sciences," in addition to whatever other disciplines the mind can reflect upon and, in turn, extrapolate into "general notions."[17] It may be argued that this definition is wholly unsatisfactory because it logically permits us to analyze historical problems and even poetry in the same manner as we attempt to solve problems in philosophy. Here the more discerning division of the subject of philosophy by Hobbes provides a clarification of Bacon's considerations.

Hobbes derived the subject matter of philosophy mostly through exclusion, whereas Bacon marked his definition by including what potentially may seem to be different criteria—the arts and sciences—but which, in fact, are not mutually exclusive. Theology, or the belief in God, is the first subject Hobbes purged from proceedings in philosophy, for "God has no parts" and only that which is conducive to "composition and resolution" may be deduced philosophically.[18] But this reasoning does not apply to the third category Hobbes rejects, history. And here we may gain an insight into Hobbes's neglect to give credit or even to recognize the authority of Bacon's teaching. His failure to account for historical circumstances, insofar as they helped to determine the course of his own thought and also because history is composed essentially of a process identifying bodies, or "experiences" of human beings as he referred to it, is a serious shortcoming. Hobbes announced the reason for prohibiting this particular factor: historical knowledge is "not ratiocination or computation."[19] Next, Hobbes set out to segregate all knowledge acquired by "Divine inspiration." Compare this with Bacon's attempt to omit the very same kind of knowledge from the vocabulary of philosophy. The dictates of reason have no application to "Inspired Divinity"; in virtue of this fact, he says, "the stars of philosophy, which have hitherto so nobly shone upon us [will no] longer supply their [Divine subjects'] light."[20] Because the last doctrine that Hobbes excluded from philosophy, the notion of a sacred God, was accounted for under the category of theology, we have only to take cognizance of his penultimate instruction, which includes propositions that are either "false" or "doubtful." If by excluding astrology, as Hobbes specifically did, he was trying to construct a sound, objective science independent of anything arbitrary or accidental, then surely this is good Baconism.

A disparity arises, however, in the fact that Bacon advocated the advancement of irrefutable knowledge but did not reject astrology as part of the arts and sciences under his illustrious philosophy. Bacon believed astrology was something more than mere superstition and went so far as to suggest that it was based on "reason and physical speculations":

To consider the matter however a little more attentively. In the first place what an idle invention is that, that each of the planets reigns in turn for an hour, so that in the space of twenty-four hours each has three reigns, leaving three hours over! And yet this conceit was the origin of our division of the week (a thing so ancient and generally received).[21]

Underlying this divergence of opinion regarding the admission-exclusion of astrology is a broader dissimilarity between Bacon's and Hobbes's approach to philosophy: Hobbes was more positive and unequivocal and, consequently, his attitude was more determined than Bacon's in the sense that he attempted to bridge any gap between philosophy and science. This can be shown in the simple manner in which Hobbes equated the two sets of problems and also coalesced moral right, physics, and geometry into one objective understanding, philosophy.

Similar to the way he ascertained the particular subjects of philosophy, Hobbes applied exclusionary precepts to define philosophy. Following a tradition laid down by Bacon and Descartes—the repudiation of sensual knowledge and the positive assertion of doubt—Hobbes rejected all immediate knowledge given to the senses.[22] Phenomena comprehended in sense certainty are categorically excluded. As Hobbes put it, "Experience concludeth nothing universally." According to Hobbes, this includes memory, which consists of a tentative appeal to the mind, experience, which is memory seemingly made concrete, and prudence, which is an expectation of a memory of experience already revealed. A more precise definition of philosophy is "science," which in itself does not tell us much about what distinguishes its component features. We are therefore left with the understanding that to philosophize is to reason ("correctly" Hobbes adds), and this means to compute. This form of reckoning is the same in all fields of investigation, whether it is logic, geometry, politics, or law. But the basic process itself remains arithmetical. "When a man *Reasoneth*," begins Hobbes in the fifth chapter of *Leviathan*,

hee does nothing else but conceive a summe totall, from *Addition* of parcels; or conceive a Remainder, from *Substraction* of one summe from another: which (if it be done by Words) is conceiving of the consequence of the names of all the parts, to the name of the whole; or from the names of the whole and one part, to the name of the other part. And though in some things, (as in numbers,) besides *Adding* and *Substracting*, men name other operations, as *Multiplying* and *Dividing*; yet they are the same; for Multiplication, is but Adding together of things equall; and Division, but Substracting of one thing, as often as we can. These operations are not incident to Numbers onely, but to all manner of things that can be added together, and taken one out of another.[23]

For Hobbes, then, science is equivalent to philosophy, whose authority is dependent upon computation. Truth, according to Hobbes, is merely getting one's sums right. But the problem of reconciling the three formal branches of knowledge—philosophy, science, and mathematics—is not as yet resolved because the possibility of mathematics as an independent form of experience still exists. The content of philosophy is meaningless without science because science mediates the object in relation to it; but what contains the matter of mathematics? Here Hobbes equates science with mathematics and thus comes full circle, resolving all domains under the heading of philosophy.

But does Hobbes follow this strict definition throughout his works, thereby disallowing any possibility to discern the presumable logic of each discourse despite their overstated close association? This is a difficult problem, which contains no obvious solution.[24] We are safe in saying that the connection between the common usage of such terms as *philosophy, knowledge, science, compendium,* and *reasoning* in the seventeenth century was close. The best example of this is Hobbes's employment of *geometry* as the "only indisputable mother of science," from which we could logically deduce, from what has just been said, that philosophy is geometry.[25] The situation, however, is noteworthy especially as it confronts continually anyone examining philosophical contexts with an eye to finding the sense or meaning of a given notion.[26]

It is not unreasonable, therefore, to conclude that Hobbes encountered philosophical inquiry as an affirmation of the principles or modes of scientific and mathematical reasoning, whereas for Bacon this relationship was in its formative stages and thus, at times, appears somewhat conditional and arbitrary. Where Bacon may be viewed as Hobbes's mentor is in designating a teleological purpose for philosophical investigation and in positing a strict correspondence between philosophy and *ratio*. The most striking dissimilarity between the two is purely biographical; Bacon was comparatively unacquainted with mathematics and many scientific experiments of his epoch, whereas Hobbes was well versed in both fields.

We are now in a position to proceed from topographical determinations of philosophy and focus our attention on the prevailing quantitative aspects of Hobbes's own theories. In general Hobbes may be read from two levels: from the realm of mechanics and from the realm of mathematics. These subdivisions, however, can be distinguished too sharply. A more careful standpoint would regard the two realms as dynamic and interacting; that is, Hobbes continuously shifted from a conception of body to the more mediate conception of ratiocination, which may, I suggest, be called a mechanico-mathematical type of reasoning.

The Road away from Babel

Certainly one of the most interesting elements of the seventeenth century was the unfailing attempt to shift terminology from the neoclassical metaphysical method of analogy to a concrete, precisely determined language. The ideal of mathematical expression, with its exactitude, colorlessness, and simple terms, appealed to a growing number of natural philosophers in the period. As Thomas Sprat observed in his *History of the Royal Society*, they had rejected

all the amplifications, digressions, and swelling of style; to return back to the primitive purity, the shortness, when men delivered for many things, almost in an equal number of words. They have exacted from all their members, a close, naked, natural way of speaking, positive expressions, clearness, a native easiness: bringing all things as near as the Mathematical plainness, as they can.[27]

The rise of a *furror mathesis* was apparently the order of the day.

Hobbes, too, was very much concerned with the problem of the rationality of language and the manner in which it could best develop. His elaborate system of definitions, particularly in *Leviathan*, attests to this conclusion. Like Bacon, Hobbes believed that language in the past had become imbued with ambitious and unclear forms. Both men were vigorously opposed to the pedantry and Aristotelian orientation of the universities in their time. Hobbes's subsequent remarks in his review of *Leviathan* reveal a writer eager to supersede the teachings of Aristotle and to transform the decayed state of language into a precise and self-contained system as accurate as the geometrical method itself.[28]

Broadly viewed, the properties of Hobbes's anatomy of language were these:

1. Speech consists of names and their connection. God was the first author of language.
2. Speech develops out of thought and acts to register its activities; both speech and thought are derived from sense.
3. The abuses of language are many; most notable are those universal names that bear no use.
4. The geometrician's language is the most indisputable; its definitions are rigidly determined.
5. Definitions are thus essential for the future possibilities of concise language; to neglect them will lead to permanently growing misconceptions.
6. To take account of names and words is simply to conceive of them as elements of *Ratiocinatio*.
7. Names can be expressed in terms of arithmetical processes, such as addition and substraction, as well as theorems and aphorisms.

Hobbes's considerations of the problem of language are found chiefly in *Elements of Philosophy* and *Leviathan*. Written four years after his discussion of the form and power of a commonwealth in *Leviathan* (1651), the *Elements* repeats in certain instances what Hobbes mentioned earlier in the significant fifth chapter, "Of Man."

Elements again raises the matter of computation and examines in greater detail the consequences that are seen to flow from it.

Hobbes began his analysis in a nominalist manner by denying the existence of "anything we call Infinite."[29] His argument was that man cannot conceive anything unless it is regarded "in some place . . . with some determinate magnitude; and which may be divided into parts." And later, he continues, "Whereas men divide a Body in their thoughts, by numbering parts of it, and in numbering those parts, number also the parts of the Place it filled; it cannot be, but in making many parts, we make also many places of those parts; whereby there cannot be conceived in the mind of any man, more, or fewer parts, than there are places for."[30] Hobbes thus conceived things existing in the first instance within the boundaries of the finite, sensible world.

But words, according to Hobbes, stem from thoughts, not things. Speech is therefore concerned with showing the relation between names and how closely a given term corresponds to its notion. It proceeds along the lines of a geometrical demonstration: first, "in apt imposing of Names," and second, "by getting a good orderly Method in proceeding from the Elements, which are Names, to Assertions made by Connection of one of them to another, till we come to a knowledge, of all the Consequence of names appertaining to the subject in hand."[31]

One further point deserves notice. Certain names, Hobbes suggests, possess more use value than others and are therefore more fruitful in the development of language. Hobbes's version of insignificant words includes *Entity, Essence,* and *Intentionality,* as well as words that are grounded on the possibility or the potentiality of their becoming realized as individual objects. This reference is directed to Aristotle.[32]

Hobbes's interest in the use of names led to the reckoning of numbers, a point overlooked by Bacon's logicism. To be sure, words are the source of logical relationships, without which it is impossible to comprehend the most basic premises of mathematics, let alone "of Magnitudes, of Swiftness, of Force, and other things, the reckonings whereof are necessary to the being, or well-being of man-kind."[33] The essential criterion of mathematics in Hobbes's epistemology comes out here once again. Hobbes derived this judgment from the Romans who first recognized the importance of accounting for their expenses.

Ratiocinatio meant the determination of some quantifiable factor, perhaps their booty. The evaluation of each item they called *nomina*, or in modern terms, *names*. But the point at issue is the fact that every name is either expressed in the language of how much or it explains nothing: "Subject to Names, is whatsoever can enter into, or be considered in an account; and be added one to another to make a summe; or substracted one from another, and leave a remainder."[34]

A clear illustration of the significance of words may be found in Hobbes's consideration of definitions. Knowledge is a process of reflecting and critically examining past definitions; those that can be proven wrong are superseded by newly discovered definitions. We may be led at this stage to interpret Hobbes as advocating the reanalysis of existing knowledge through recourse to experience. New experiments dispose us to reject former discoveries. This is not, however, what Hobbes was suggesting.[35] The special quality of mathematical investigation is that it is an act of the mind. Finding the right definition of names, Hobbes concludes, "is to be done only by arguments and ratiocination."[36]

For Hobbes, the process of forming propositions is also analogous to arithmetic reasoning, and irrespective of the misconception by some scholars that Hobbes's characterization of propositions represents an "ontological departure" from Aristotle's framework, the fact is that there exists a close affinity between them in this instance.[37] For Aristotle, a proposition is formed by the addition of another term. Hence it follows that "a different conclusion comes about if an additional immediate proposition is taken."[38] For example, we may say, (1) "He is a child," (2) "He is afraid," and (3) "He is an afraid child." All three examples are propositions because they bring one entity or name into contact with another. Proposition 3, however, consists of qualities the same as propositions 1 and 2, but because of its added element it connotes a completely different meaning. Essentially the same logical format is involved in Hobbes's reasoning: "In every proposition, three things are to be considered, viz. the two names, which are the subject and the predicate, and their copulation."[39]

Aristotle also plays a somewhat important role in the later stages of Hobbes's conception of propositions. Each new proposition, from Aristotle's point of view, is intelligible only by reference to its being a whole or a part. The universal meant for Aristotle "what can be predicated of more than one thing," that is, that which can be translated into quantities.[40] A particular proposition, on the contrary, is limited to a single object; one does not quantify or attribute "all" or "of so many" to describe or prove it. Hobbes's propositions correspond to Aristotle's in that they are distinguished by their quantity or their quality. Propositions of the former sort are founded on the grounds that they express very general truth values. For instance, in the proposition, "Every man is a living creature," we attain the highest level of universality. The qualitative distinction of a proposition emphasizes its particular and exclusive characteristics. The statement "Man is a living creature" recognizes distinct and heterogenic factors.

If there is an essentially novel feature in Hobbes's consideration of logistic propositions, it rests in his distinction between true and false propositions. The idea of a true proposition depends on the building up of its component parts such that each becomes equivalent to one another. According to Hobbes, the proposition, "Man is a living creature," constitutes a true order because "man" and "living creature" are identical. Each name possesses a partial character, and its similitude with another word unites them both into a moment of truth.

The Role and Definition of Quantity and Its Connection to Virtue

It is a notable comment on Hobbes "that he was wont to draw lines on his thighs and on the sheets, abed, and also multiply and divide."[41] This is probably the most intimate and private statement we have about Hobbes and doubtless to some psychoanalysts, the most revealing as well. But the full importance of this rumor is not unveiled until we move from the world of idle gossip and observation to that of more serious discourse.

Hobbes began *The Elements of Philosophy* with the fundamental assertion that number belongs to everything in the material world and consequently cannot be understood otherwise than in terms of quantity. Extending Pythagoras's symbolic representation of number as the source of things, Hobbes emphasizes, "We must not therefore think that computation, that is, ratiocination, has place only in numbers, as if man were distinguished from other living creatures . . . by nothing but the faculty of numbering; for *magnitude, body, motion, time, degrees of quality, action, conception, proportion, speech and names* (in which all kinds of philosophy consist) are capable of addition and substraction."[42] Thus whereas the Pythagoreans stressed the figure-like order (the countableness) of the "heavens" and of "nature," Hobbes spoke of a number structure or fundamental order that belongs to the constitutive elements of philosophy. That these particular properties belonging to philosophy exhibited a countable condition as such is the conceptualization underpinning Hobbes's whole interpretation. From this standpoint Hobbes deduced that all discourse, in fact all phenomena and types of behavior, are reducible to fundamental elements, which give rise to complete clarity and no insoluble problem. The full range of the significance of this level of thought cannot be appreciated without coming face to face with one of its crucial aspects: quantity.

Like Bacon, Hobbes discussed the role and identity of quantity and its connection to determining the virtue of an object or action. The central problem here concerns the designation of a particular determined quantity and specifying the character of an individual thing or experience. As Bacon boldly asserted, "Quantity was the Dose of Nature"; he later concluded that the "Dose" he referred to meant "the quantity of body." Perhaps unconscious of Bacon's authority, Hobbes stressed the fact quite in accordance with the lord chancellor: "Quantity is nothing else but the Determination of Matter; that is to say of Body, by which we say one Body is greater, or lesser than another, by this, or this much."[43] The idea that a given body may be represented by determinate quantities is significant and should be emphasized.[44] It played an important part in Hobbes's attack on the so-called "vain philosophy of Aristotle" on the grounds that it fell into the "Error of Separated Essence," thereby failing to attribute a quantity to only corporeal substances.[45]

A quantity, to be sure, is completely determinate in the sense that it contains one or several definite units.[46] Put another way, a quantity cannot be made intelligible by an opposite because it is a unit itself. What Aristotle viewed within the realm of more or less had little relevance to Hobbes. According to Hobbes, the particular mode or virtue of a body depends upon its quantity. The central question, therefore, remains one of proportion by which a body is either equal to or different from another by so many units as such. The same proportions, of course, are not applicable to the same kinds of virtues; an inquiry that determines the proportion of virtue in a bottle of wine is unlikely to be conducive to measuring the matter of a ship or the capacity of a political regime to exercise its authority. Hence the mode of virtue differs but not the general attitude toward deciphering the significance or quantity corresponding to a substance. In any case, the virtue of a thing is a quantitative determination in the sense that it consists of a certain amount. It is useless to press this point much further. In Hobbes's "Six Lessons to the Professors of Mathematics," he expressed conclusively that quantity was an unavoidable feature in discerning what we seem to know from what is essentially to be known: "There is therefore to everything concerning which a man may ask without absurdity, *how* much *it is*, a certain quantity belonging, determining the magnitude to be *so much*. Also wheresoever there is *more* or *less*, there is no kind of quantity or other. And first there is quantity of bodies."[47]

Apart from determining the character of an object, quantity is a necessary ingredient to produce any given effect. What this signifies is that in the generation or construction of things, the effects that are produced are conditioned by the rules laid down or presupposed by a structure. As Hobbes claims, "I here undertake no more than to deliver the elements of that science by which the effects of anything may be found out from the known generation of the same, or contrarily, the generation from the effects; to the end that they who search after other philosophy, may be admonished to seek it from other principles."[48] Keeping in mind Hobbes's previous statements to the effect that a causal factor is incomprehensible without an agent and without a quantitative attribute, this much, at least, can be understood from the preceding passage: whatever effect is produced will also possess a so-called determination of matter or quantity.

The concept of quantity is of crucial importance to Hobbes. In addition, however, is the extension of the realm of applicability of quantity to the material of philosophy, which represents a specific transformation from previous tendencies that viewed such an approach as entirely unapprehensive.[49]

The Position of Magnitude and Measure

If everything belonging to the corporeal order depends on quantity, what does Hobbes believe to be the most important attribute of measure? Early in *Leviathan* (part 1, chapter 2), Hobbes made the necessary connection between a quantity to be measured and what is to be its measure or standard. Here he expressed the idea that for man to retain a state of peace in which there is no agent threatening him, consented self-defense by all men is the only condition that can secure this safety: "For men measure, not only other men, but all things, by themselves: and because they find themselves subject after motion and pain, and lassitude, think every thing else grows weary of Motion, and seeks repose of its own accord."[50] Prior to the supposed situation in which society is based on the protection of the lives of its members is what Hobbes referred to as "the bare state of nature." In this condition, there exist perpetual disputes, suspicions, wars, and other major upheavals, for it is the natural proclivity of men, says Hobbes, to destroy each other. The classical doctrine of *Homo mensura* (man is the measure of all things) is everywhere applicable in this naked and oppressive state of nature. Hobbes, however, struck a cautionary note here, adding that in a state of nature "profit is the measure of right."[51]

In a state of nature in which there are no mutually agreed-to laws binding the activities of the individuals who compose it, there is also no guideline or determined order by which to judge these actions except for the measure of "appetites." "But in a Commonwealth," declares Hobbes, "this measure is false: not the Appetite of Private men, but the Law, which is the Will and Appetite of the State is the measure."[52]

It is possible to regard such an interpretation of Hobbes as too dependent on a literate conceptualization of his use of the word *measure*. As we have learned elsewhere, one name can signify a number of different attributes. Let us therefore consider other ways in which Hobbes employs the concept of measurement to see whether my suppositions interpreting the importance of quantification are valid.

In the first part of *De Corpore*, Hobbes brings out the particular and concrete object he set for the art of philosophy. As he develops it, the relationship between measurement in general and the new ends of philosophy seem inextricably linked together. In Hobbes's view, "The greatest commodities of mankind are the arts; namely, of measuring matter and motion; of moving ponderous bodies, of architecture; of navigation; of making instruments for all uses; of calculating the celestial motions, the aspects of the stars, and the parts of time."[53]

These activities, different as they at first appear, all admit of gradations in themselves and must appeal to quantitative analyses. In placing such heavy emphasis on quantitative features, Hobbes is showing that these activities are rule governed and presuppose starting points or measures in order to be understood. But Hobbes's extension of measurable forms is limited not only to the subjects of geometry and natural bodies. Hobbes also interpreted the relation between individual men and society as calculable in terms of value. According to Hobbes, "The *Value*, or *Worth* of a man, is as all other things, his Price; that is to say, so much as would be given for the use of his Power."[54] This distinction of man as an indifferent element in the development of labor foreshadowed the principles of English political economy enunciated by Smith, Ricardo, and Mill. Hobbes regarded the determination of value as an external relationship insofar as it was "esteemed" and "needed" by others.[55] This relation thus follows closely along the development of supply and demand movements. However qualified or virtuous a man may believe himself to be, the reality is that "the buyer determines the Price," which focuses the attention away from man himself to processes and judgments settled outside him. Hobbes draws another important distinction: that man is also measured by values assigned him by society.[56] Man's value is thus the product of a dual determination: by private individuals who have a definite voice in one's worth according to the interest or productive powers that can be derived from labor, and according to special resolves of the state. The one bears a distinct mark of being an economic proportion extraneous to man himself, whereas the latter is not so much determined by demand but simply by society whenever it may deem it desirable (or in its interests) to confer a "dignity" upon one of its members.

Hobbes did not develop further the assertion that a man's value is a product of his labor, which could not be measured except by an employer who was going to determine it in terms of a sum total relation between wages and work.[57] As it stands, however, we can appreciate his insights.

I have suggested that the key principle to Hobbes's account of measurement and magnitude, as applied to the individual members of a civil society, is essentially quantitative. There are no qualitative differences between men in Hobbes's view; "men by nature [are] equal," declares Hobbes, adding that "strength of body, experience, reason, and passion, are common to all men."[58] There is, however, an even lower common denominator between men: the ability to kill each other. This is so because even "the weakest has strength enough to kill the strongest."[59] For Hobbes, then, human nature is prone to the active exertion of differences in strength and power, of individuals maximizing their own appetites and, at the same time, decreasing the risk of either death or the imposition of others' wills upon their own liberty. In order to understand this viewpoint in its full significance, we must turn to Hobbes's presentation of the foundation of a safe and relatively free civil society and to the realm of mathematics as the most precise, detached, and exemplary source of this conception.

The Alliance between Geometry and Politics

Hobbes and Galileo became friends in 1635 while Hobbes was on a trip to Florence. Aubrey relates that Hobbes "extremely venerated and magnified" the teachings of Galileo, which can be viewed as close evidence to the significant ways that Hobbes abstracted from the Galilean perspective.[60] One might say that the mathematical applications of Hobbes had a significance of its own quite apart from the natural-scientific spheres Galileo was concerned with. The difference can be understood as a transformation from a mathematized view of nature to the introduction of *geometrico* theories of human behavior. This does not suggest that mathematical investigations became more pressing than inquiries into the exact sciences. Indeed at the beginning of the seventeenth century, during Bacon's lifetime, concentration was directed mainly to the physical sciences at the expense of mathematical specializations that sprang to life during the period of Hobbes's studies. As Hobbes suggested rather boastfully, he became "the first that hath made the grounds of geometry firm and coherent."[61] Hobbes was clear, however, that "such writers or disputes thereof, as are ignorant of geometry, do but make their readers and hearers lose their time."[62]

What characterizes Hobbes's unquestioned attitude toward mathematics is a combination of two elements: the formula and quantitative function of its structure and the general truths and results it produced. The first category takes into account a process of operation, and the second is specifically concerned with performance.

In a number of places, Hobbes stated that the mathematical model is the best foundation for accomplishing the tasks of formulating a "solid philosophy" and a "sound commonwealth." Apart from William Petty, he was alone in making this proclamation.[63] His conviction stemmed from the genuine conclusions offered by this science. He wrote, for example, in *De Cive*, "For were the nature of human actions as distinctly known, as the nature of quantity in geometrical figures, the strength of avarice and ambition, which is sustained by the erroneous opinions of the vulgar, as touching the nature of right and wrong, would presently faint and languish: and mankind should enjoy such an immortal peace."[64] But the most explicit version of this judgment appears even earlier in *The Elements of Law*, written not long after his visit to Italy. He says:

[Corresponding to] the two principal parts of our nature, Reason and Passion have proceeded two kinds of learning, mathematical and dogmatical. The former is free from controversies and dispute, because it consisteth in comparing figures and motion only; in which things truth and the interest of men oppose not each other. But in the later there is nothing not disputable, because it compareth men, and meddleth with their right and profit . . . to reduce this doctrine to the rules and infallability of reason, there is no way, but first to put such principles down for a foundation as passion not mistrusting, may not seek to displace.[65]

Above all else, Hobbes clearly showed his desire to orient political philosophy according to the principles of mathematics, although he does not tell us the means in which it was thus applied. Here we must step back to our first point, the manner or method whereby mathematics exhibits its exactness; only then can we understand fully the way in which Hobbes sought to apply it to his political theory.

The necessity and consequences of determining a proper method of inquiry cannot easily be pushed aside. By and large, the importance of method dominated thinking in this period.[66] Attention has been drawn already to Bacon's overriding concern with the matter.[67] To be sure, methodic reasoning was especially part of the necessary equipment of mathematics and was thus declared an exemplary discipline from the outset by such writers as Stevin, Descartes, and Hobbes.

As far as he had become acquainted with it, Stevin claimed that "I have not noted any better for the matter of mathematics than the wise age [the age of the moderns]."⁶⁸ This thesis is even more clearly advanced in Descartes. In his opinion, "of all the sciences known as yet, arithmetic and geometry alone are free from any taint of falsity or uncertainty."⁶⁹ The elements of these two sciences that Descartes appears to stress are the criteria of truth and the demonstrative certainty that they yield. As Descartes himself pointed out in *A Discourse on Method, mathesis universalis* derives its starting point in the purely symbolic conceptions the "naked intellect" represents. Thus a "master-calculator" is able to separate or abstract things of quantity from the content-bearing substance itself and yet retain the truth of the subject by means of its imaginary dimensions. The distinction between intellect and sense data becomes important here when we realize that Descartes's division of these two realms was a consequence of his assertion that the principles of mathematics did not depend on phenomena of sensation; nor, for that matter, did mathematical demonstrations.

It remains open how much Hobbes owes to this specifically new attachment to methodological considerations. In any case, Hobbes's clearest treatment of the matter appears in the beginning of *De Corpore*. In effect, contends Hobbes, "Every man brought Philosophy, that is, Natural Reason, into the world with him; for all men can reason to some degree, and concerning some things: but where there is need of a long series of reasons, there men wander out of the way, and fall into error for want of method."⁷⁰ Hobbes is presenting us here with something that goes beyond mere addition and subtraction.⁷¹

The chief object of Hobbes's mathematical orientation is to come to terms not with the direct study of numbers themselves or kinds of figures. Rather he attempts to comprehend the variety of human and physical arrangements under determinate, well-defined properties that possess definite and unambiguous relations to the things or material that underlie them. This means that knowing as mere counting is opposed to the presentation of a guidepost or procedural operation whereby objects may be treated as countable and delimited as such. The first enables us simply to account for units in whatsoever manner we wish, whereas the second allows us to compare and find the unity, similarity, and proportions of two or more things with each other.⁷² For Hobbes the ability of man to calculate and to enumerate things in question becomes meaningful only if, through this source, other knowledge that treats of mathematical classifications and description can be gained.[73] Thus ratiocination attains its real significance only with reference to other fields of study besides *arithmos* itself. We shall see this particularly displayed insofar as Hobbes's special posture of the new political science is concerned. But before dealing with the way in which Hobbes makes mathematics accessible to political understanding, a few remarks are needed to set forth the largely well-known character of mathematical knowledge.

According to mathematical thinking, the whole is always more known than the parts. The preliminary discovery of the parts is obtained only if we have an expressly formulated rule to proceed from. Figures and the properties exhibited in figures (such as the sides of a rectangle) grow initially out of these rules but are merely images or points marked in space. As such they are founded or understood as consecutive acts of reasoning. Theorems thus grow out of prefigured statements without which we would be infinitely searching for particular causalities "floating in the air." In order to grasp fully the concrete and particular content involved, we constantly refer to or measure our demonstrations against the original assumption.

What really mattered for Hobbes was that we should determine commonwealths and norms according to this procedure of reasoning. Mathematics was considered universally applicable. Therefore the task was to apply men's actions so that a consistency or pattern could be reached according to preestablished rules governing commonwealths.[74] These laws were neither accidently nor arbitrarily chosen; rather they were primary definitions that "are either known by themselves, or else they are not principles." "Naturally given," they were inviolable commands directing social relations in the same way that natural bodies conformed to the regularities of motion.

Hobbes presumed that the principal rule of human behavior is to seek peace; "all the rest of the laws are merely means to obtain this result."[75] All actions therefore must conform to this solitary precept before other questions of social action can be determined. He also recommended in this connection that practice alone is not an acceptable assurance upon which the rules of governing can be based.[76] This is an important concept because it shows that the generality of the formal rules he established extends beyond both precedents and trends into the domain of accurately predictable facts of law. The fundamental traits of geometry are thus transferable to civil society insofar as criteria upon which both are based can be demonstrated within the framework of preregulated axioms.[77]

The relationship of norms and mathematics is by no means indifferent to exact definition, and here it may be illustrative to consider Hobbes's juxtaposition of commutative and distributive justice.[78] Here too, Hobbes expressed his premises within the context of mathematics and concluded that commutative justice is not distinct from arithmetic, whereas distributive justice is accounted for by the useful tenets of geometry. From what has already been said about Hobbes's disposition to set out his political philosophy as closely aligned with the whole of mathematics as possible, this hardly comes as a surprising judgment. But if we bear in mind the classical concepts of justice, we find a sharp contrast between Hobbes and the Aristotelian and Platonic traditions.[79] It was natural for the classical philosophers to identify justice with wisdom and to oppose it to piety. So considered, it became a principle of logic that expressed the best account of man's position with respect to society. Plato's just division of labor in his *Republic* is an eloquent testimonial to this condition. The classical theories were founded, according to Hobbes, on a misleading hypothesis: that in existence and participation man is a "political animal." Hobbes's objection, especially in *De Cive*, is that the notion of man as a political and social being is purely a guise; he interprets the natural inclination of man as seeking personal gain and honor. Consequently the boundary lines between the two forms of justice needed to be reestablished.

What, then, distinguishes distributive from commutative justice? According to Hobbes, distributive justice is a question of proportion whereby commodities, civil rights, benefits, and honors, are divided among the population. It is well known that in any society this distribution may be made with the intention of equality, but, ironically, virtue, merit, and status imply inequality. It would be ridiculous therefore to reduce distributive shares to a binding order. Conversely the essential form of commutative justice is that an equality of value can be rendered for things mutually contracted for between individuals. The justice being dispensed with here deals "in exchanging, in buying, selling, borrowing, lending, location and conduction, and other acts whatsoever belonging to contractors."[80]

The ultimate end in the two kinds of justice is to increase the quantity of value, or, put another way, to minimize the amount of one's loss. From either vantage point, the individual is differentiated in the state less according to need, adequacy, and capacity than the ability to generate an ample profit or supply of goods, corresponding to economic transactions, and steady attention from other human beings, representing distributive relations. Thus they differ not so much in degree as in substance.

One might further add that Hobbes conceived justice as right reason, which was a matter of reckoning—through addition, subtraction, and demonstration—the sum of men's duties in civil life. Nowhere does Hobbes assert that justice is contrary to reason or that it is a condition of realizing any sort of ideal scheme. It is obvious that Hobbes's discourse on the nature of justice is unintelligible without the mathematical peculiarities. Those who read Hobbes as primarily concerned with justice as an important ontological category—in which case the element of mathematics may be considered a *quantité négligeable*—miss the whole spirit of demonstrable, questionless, and infallibly reliable conclusions that he offered.

Notes

1. John Aubrey, *Brief Lives*, ed. Andrew Clark (Oxford, 1848), vol. 1, p. 331.

2. Ibid.

3. Hobbes, *English Works*, ed. W. Molesworth (London, 1839), vol. 4, p. 317, vol. 21, p. 112 (hereafter referred to as *EW*).

4. See the introductory remarks on Bacon in chapter 2.

5. Frithiof Brandt, *Thomas Hobbes' Mechanical Conception of Nature* (London, 1928).

6. Ibid., p. 58.

7. Alfred North Whitehead, *The Interpretation of Science* (New York, 1961), p. 33.

8. See Bacon, *Philosophical Works*, ed. J. M. Robertson (London, 1905), p. 323 (aphorism xx) (hereafter referred to as *PW*).

9. Ibid. (aphorism x1).

10. Hobbes, *EW*, vol. 4, p. 309.

11. M. Samuel Sorbriére, *Voyage en Angleterre* (London, 1709), pp. 31–32.

12. Gaston Sortas, *La philosophie moderne depuis Bacon jusqu'a*

Leibniz (Paris, 1920), pp. 426–27. See also Frischeisen-Kohler, *Die Natur-philosophie de Th. Hobbes in ihrer Abhanggezkeit von Bacon*, Archiv Bd. XV, pp. 370 ff, quoted in Brandt, *Hobbes' Mechanical Conception*, p. 56, who considers Bacon as a precursor to Hobbes's "Little Treatise" (1630 c).

13. See Neal W. Gilbert, *Renaissance Concepts of Method* (New York, 1960), p. 224.

14. See Bacon, *PW*, pp. 60, 94, 259 (aphorism ii).

15. Hobbes, *Elements of Philosophy*, in *EW*, vol. 1, p. 7.

16. Hobbes, *EW*, vol. 1, p. 7; Bacon, *PW*, p. 259 (aphorism iii).

17. See Bacon, "Descriptio Globi Intellectualis," *PW*, p. 677.

18. Hobbes, *EW* vol. 4, p. 307.

19. Ibid., pp. 3–7.

20. Bacon, "De Augmentis," in *PW*, p. 631.

21. Ibid., p. 462.

22. See ibid., pp. 99–100, (aphorism lxviii), 288 (aphorism xcvii); Descartes, *Discourse on Method and the Meditations*, trans, F. E. Sutcliffe (Middlesex, 1968), passim.

23. Hobbes, *Leviathan*, Everyman's ed. (New York, 1973), p. 18; Hobbes, *EW*, vol. 1, p. 3.

24. The significance of Hobbes's blended form of mathematics and mechanics cannot be overrated. I repeat it here because his philosophy seems inapprehensible without the certain and indisputable procedures furnished by those fields of study. The immediate influence or specific source of Hobbes's mathematical-physical studies is of less importance to us here than the fact that the distinction among mathematics, science, and philosophy is considerably obliterated by him. Just how difficult it is to draw the boundaries between them can be seen, for example, in Hobbes's words in the *Leviathan*: "Science, that is, knowledge of consequences; which is called also Philosophy" (p. 42); "The true Mother of them [i.e., the sciences] be Science, namely the Mathematiques" (p. 44); "For Nature worketh by Motion; the ways, and Degrees whereof cannot be known, without the knowledge of the Proportions and Properties of Lines and Figures" (p. 366).

25. Ibid., pp. 15, 20, 365.

26. See J. W. Watkin's treatment of this in *Hobbes' System of Ideas* (London, 1965), chap. 8.

27. Thomas Sprat, *History of the Royal Society* (London, p. 113). See also R. Boyle, *Works*, ed. T. Birch (London, 1744), vol. 1, p. 22, where he expresses a similar idea: "I conceive no impossibility," he says, "that opposes the doing that in words, that we see already done in numbers."

28. See Hobbes, *Leviathan*, p. 391.

29. Ibid., p. 11.

30. Ibid., p. 370.

31. Ibid., p. 21.

32. Ibid., pp. 12, 369.

33. Ibid., p. 15.

34. Ibid., p. 216.

35. "For if experimentations of natural phenomena are to be called philosophy, then pharmacists are the greatest physicians of all." Hobbes, *EW*, vol. 4, p. 228.

36. Ibid., p. 28.

37. See, for example, Thomas A. Spragens, Jr., *The Politics of Motion* (London, 1973), p. 141.

38. See Aristotle, *Posterior Analytics*, trans. Jonathan Barnes (Oxford, 1975) 88b6, 88b19.

39. Hobbes, *EW*, vol. 1, p. 31.

40. Aristotle, *Metaphysics*, in *The Works of Aristotle*, ed. W. D. Ross (Oxford, 1925) 1038b11.

41. Aubrey, *Brief Lives*, p. 309.

42. Hobbes, *EW*, vol. 1, p. 5.

43. Hobbes, *Leviathan*, p. 371. Compare Bacon: "Almost all particular virtues act according to the greater or less quantity of the body." Bacon, *PW*, p. 365.

44. "All bodies therefore differ from one another in number." Hobbes, *EW*, vol. 1, p. 133.

45. See Hobbes, *Leviathan*, p. 369.

46. See Aristotle, *Metaphysics*, vol. 1, 1052b22ff.

47. Hobbes, *EW*, vol. 7, p. 193.

48. Ibid., vol. 1, p. 12.

49. See, for example, Aristotle, *Ethics*, 1094b12, 1098b5.

50. Hobbes, *Leviathan*, p. 44.

51. Hobbes, *De Cive*, ed. Sterling P. Lamprecht (New York, 1949), p. 28.

52. Hobbes, *Leviathan*, p. 372.

53. Hobbes, *De Corpore*, ed. Ferdinand Tönnies (Cambridge, 1928), chaps. 1, 7.

54. Hobbes, *Leviathan*, p. 44.

55. Ibid.

56. Ibid.

57. This is, to be sure, an essential feature of any modern capitalist enterprise. It might also be pointed out that my argument to the effect that this notable criterion of capitalist production is absent in Hobbes's assumption is at odds with C. B. MacPherson's characterization of the Hobbesian competitive market society. See his *The Political Theory of Possessive Individualism: Hobbes to Locke* (Oxford, 1962), p. 53ff.

58. Hobbes, *EW*, vol. 4, pp. 81, 105, vol. 1, p. 133.

59. Hobbes, *Leviathan*, p. 63.

60. Aubrey, *Brief Lives*, p. 366.

61. Hobbes, *EW* vol. 7, p. 242. This is typical, although quite wrong, of Hobbes's egocentric evaluation of his own work. Descartes's *Geometrica*, for instance, was published by Van Schooter in 1649 in addition to his *Principles of Universal Mathematics or An Introduction to the Method of Geometry* (first edition in 1651); furthermore, Descartes's geometric formations had been anticipated by Stevin in his *Arithmétique* (first edition in 1585). See *The Principal Works of Simon Stevin*, vol. 2, ed. E. J. Dijkaterhuis, R. J. Forbes, M. G. Minnaert, and A. Pannekock (Amsterdam, 1955–1961); A. G. Kästner, *Geschichte der Mathematik* (Göttinger, 1799), vol. 3, pp. 111–52.

62. Hobbes, *EW*, vol. 1, p. 73. Hobbes is obviously referring to Plato in this instance. See Plato, *The Protagoras*, trans. W. K. C. Gutherie, in *Collected Dialogues*, 346C, and *Euthyphro*, trans. L. Cooper, in *Collected Dialogues*, 7B–C.

63. The primary reference that supports this assertion is James Harrington, *The Common-Wealth of Oceana* (London, 1656).

64. Hobbes, *De Cive*, p. 3.

65. Hobbes, *The Elements of Law*, ed. Ferdinand Tönnies (London, 1889), p. xv.

66. For the importance of method in more modern analyses of social and political problems, see, for example, Auguste Comte, *Cours de philosophie positive* (Paris, 1830–1842), vol. 2, p. 210, where he points out, "In every science, conceptions which relate to method are incomparable from those which relate to the doctrine under consideration."

67. See "The Great Instauration," in *PW*, pp. 402–408.

68. Stevin, *Principal Works*, vol. 2, p. 110.

69. Descartes, "Rules for the Direction of the Mind," in *Philosophical Works*. See also the letter of March 26, 1619, to Beeckman where he speaks of a *scientia penitus nova* (a totally new science) "by which all problems which can be proposed in terms of any kind of quantity, whether continuous or discrete, can be generally solved."

70. Hobbes, *EW*, vol. 1, p. 1; Hobbes, *Leviathan*, p. 364. Hobbesian scholars are wont to stress the resoluto-compositive method of analysis as Hobbes's principal contribution to rationalizing theories of civil philosophy. On this method see *EW*, vol. 1, p. 66, and Hobbes, *De Corpore*, 1, vi, 1; also Marino Ghetaldi, *De resolutione et compositione mathematica* (1630). The following modern works are also relevant. Watkins, *Hobbes' System of Ideas*, chap. 4; Richard Peters, *Hobbes* (Harmondsworth, 1956), chap. 2; F. S. McNeilly, *The Anatomy of Leviathan* (London, 1968), chap. 4. In my opinion Hobbes, unlike Descartes, for example, uses the terms in question

rather promiscuously and never expressly states which method has priority or best corresponds to his treatment of civil philosophy. On the one hand, he says that politics can be synthetically deduced from a long chain of reasoning beginning with *philosophia prima*, geometry, arithmetic, astronomy, and others, culminating with ethics, poetry, rhetoric, logic, and finally politics. Hobbes, *De Corpore*, 1, vi, 7, and *Leviathan*, p. 42. On the other hand he says that the propositions of politics are universally established and self-evident "even to the meanest capacity." Hobbes, *De Corpore* 1, xii, 3, and *EW*, vol. 3, pp. 23, 358. I have therefore abandoned this designation in favor of a more simplistic account of Hobbes's theses, which attempts to deal with the objects and connectedness of his presuppositions.

71. And also distinctly beyond the Platonic dictum that the superiority of man over animal life consists in the fact "that he alone knows how to count." See Plato, *Laws*, 818C, *Republic*, 522E; also Hobbes's statement in *Leviathan*, p. 364, where he says, "The savages of America are not without some good Morall Sentences; also they have, a little Arithmetick, to adde, and divide in Numbers not too great: but they are not therefore Philosophers." And as Hobbes points out in the verse poem of his *Vita* (London, 1679): "my book *De Corpore* . . . Whose Matter's wholly Geometrical."

72. The role played in mathematical conceptions by comparison is too often overlooked. In mathematics proper, it refers to ascertaining how much one magnitude or quantity either exceeds or is contained in the other. In logic it distinguishes relations between propositions; uncertain propositions are compared with certain propositions. Indeed the way in which Hobbes distinguishes the "causes or generation" and "effects or appearance" of things from each other is largely a product of this kind of reasoning. See Hobbes, *EW*, pp. 3, 12, 121–22; *Elements of Law*, p. xv. See also Plato, *Theaeteus*, 186B and Descartes, "Rules for the Direction of the Mind," rules VI, XVIII.

73. In a negative sense, Hobbes has in mind here the exclusion of theology or "the doctrine of God" because "there is nothing to divide nor compound, nor any generation to be conceived." Hobbes, *De Corpore*, 1, i, 8, 10.

74. See Hobbes, *Leviathan*, p. 110.

75. Hobbes, *De Cive*, p. 52.

76. "The skill of making, and maintaining Common-wealth, consisteth in certain Rules, as doth Arithmetique and Geometry; not (as Tennis-play) on Practice only." Hobbes, *Leviathan*, p. 110.

77. This shows most clearly the close connection between mathematics and civil society; both emerge from the intelligence (factors localized within us), whereas the material of physics is largely conjectural and external in character. Cf. Leo Strauss, *The Political Philosophy of Hobbes* (Oxford, 1936), p. 137.

78. See Hobbes, *De Cive*, p. 46, *Leviathan*, pp. 77ff, *Elements of Law*, p. 84, *De Corpore*, in *EW*, vol. 4, pp. 97–98. See also the views of Jean Bodin on geometric, arithmetic, and harmonic types of justice, in *The Six Bookes of a Commonweale*, ed. Kenneth McRae (Cambridge, Mass., 1962), pp. 755ff.

79. Hobbes's remarks here are probably best understood in the context of a polemic against, in particular, Aristotle's concept of justice. See Aristotle, *Ethics*, bk. III, H, 3–5, and *Leviathan*, pp. 78, 366. What especially characterizes Hobbes's "new" conception of the two forms of justice is, first, his dismissal of Aristotle's distributive notion of "awards according to merit"; for Hobbes it is not unjust "to sell dearer than we buy; or to give more to a man than he merits" (p. 78); and second, his subordination of the old concept of remedial or commutative justice as an equal and commensurate exchange relation to one in which the "Contractor" or buyer determines the just price or how much he may be "contented to give" (pp. 44, 78).

80. Hobbes, *Leviathan*, p. 78.

4

Quantitative Components in Mill

> I have no faith in anything
> short of actual measurement
> and the rule of three.
> —*Darwin*

More than most of his predecessors, as well as his contemporaries, John Stuart Mill was extremely well versed in mathematical and scientific studies. Born in 1806, the eldest son of the philosopher James Mill, he was privately tutored throughout his childhood by his father, a conscientious, dedicated man who was considerably successful in bestowing a formal intellectual education upon his children. As Mill's autobiographical recollections reveal, "the only thing besides Greek" that his father made him learn at the age of three, "was arithmetic."[1] At eight he began studying Euclid's *Elements*, and soon afterward he was learning the principles of algebra. By his twelfth year, his formal mathematical exercises included differential calculus, a subject that Mill himself says he never seriously mastered. Throughout these years, Mill had placed great emphasis on experimental science, which he later viewed as one of the "greatest amusements" during his up-bringing. As we learn from his *Autobiography*, the young Mill "devoured treatises on Chemistry" and argued vociferously against his father's criticisms of a leading scientific textbook.[2]

In addition to his courses on mathematics and science, Mill commenced learning logic at the age of twelve. His first lessons included Aristotle's logical works, collectively called the *Organon*, and in particular, *Posterior Analytics*; the latter was neither intelligible nor interesting to Mill at this early stage of cultivation, despite the fact that Aristotle's logic later provided the nucleus for Mill's own attempt at a formal and systematic presentation of the assumptions of logical in-quiry. From this study followed an analysis of Hobbes's "Computatio sive Logica," whose corpus, or system, Mill admired less than did his father. Mill's impressive childhood training had a profound effect on much of his scholarship. As he wrote, "I started, I may fairly say, with an advantage of a quarter of a century over my contemporaries."[3]

Central to Mill's theoretical framework is the belief that the so-called moral sciences were in a very "backward state." Previous achievements had been barren and had failed to grasp the truth of sci-entific discovery and explanation. Future formulations could remedy this situation only by applying "the methods of physical science, duly extended and generalized."[4] This much, at least, Mill shared with Comte, Condorcet, Turgot, and the positivist system of thought in general.[5] Especially interesting is Mill's statement in his *Autobiog-raphy* that he arrived at the belief that "the methods of physical science [were] the proper models for political" understanding before he had encountered either the St. Simonians or Comte's work.[6]

Mill regarded himself in a position to reorganize the decayed and fruitless conceptions of human knowledge, particularly since Bacon's time,[7] "on a [firm] basis of analyzed experience, in opposition to the theory of innate principles."[8] Accordingly he maintained that the canons, explanations, and underlying structure of the sciences could be expounded in well-defined language and cogently formalized. "In this respect," says Mill in book 5 of his *System of Logic*, "mathe-matics are only on a par with most other sciences."[9] The tradition, stretching as far back as Plato, claiming the priority, independence, and "intellectual dominance" of mathematics, was thus attacked by Mill.[10] This is not to suggest that Mill wholly ignored mathematics; rather he sought to tailor its influence by demonstrating that "moral and social phenomena . . . can be made instrumental to the forma-tion of a similar body of received doctrine in moral and political science."[11]

Mill took some pains to show that the properties of logic, above all else, exhibit the same certainty as found in mathematical theory. Both branches of inquiry, he said, at bottom are equivalent in the sense that they are both concerned with ascertaining the accuracy of particular propositions and the consequences or results thereof. Further, both approaches attempt a proof, a proposition or assertion that denies or affirms what is inferred or signified in it. For example, the proposition, "Every triangle has angles equal to two right angles," contains assumptions, the truth or falseness of which can be determined through either the use of mathematical theorems or logical inferences. As Mill emphasized, "To reason is simply to infer any assertion from assertions already admitted; and in this sense induction is as much entitled to be called reasoning as the demonstrations of geometry."[12]

Mill is therefore offering guidance to historians, philosophers, and researchers in any other branch of human knowledge. Each body of truth, according to Mill, admits of some exactness. The essential exercise is to uncover this certainty and precision by means of a logical scientific method. This attitude implies that a science of human affairs, which makes human behavior subject to invariable laws, is possible; previous efforts of this sort have proven unsuccessful; and the procedure and method of investigation proposed anew is correct and can be applied to human nature.

Methods of Inquiry

Mill's preoccupation with the perennial proper method of understanding the uniformities and similarities assigned to phenomena occurred when he was just beginning to reexamine the validity of the vast body of opinions he was imbued with: Benthamism and his father's psychological associationism. Despite the fact that he never completely rejected the basic assertions underlying the Benthamite or utilitarian explanations of cognition and action, Mill nevertheless scrutinized and demonstrated the errors in its methodology. As he pointed out in his *Autobiography*, the appearance of Thomas Macaulay's article in the *Edinburgh Review* (1829) attacking his father's *Essay on Government* "gave me much to think about."[13] Macaulay's study was aimed more at renouncing James Mill's method than the ideas and prognostications that developed from it. He claimed that the elder Mill had erred in deducing laws of human nature that cannot be proven necessary or determinate in all cases. In place of this abstract geometric approach, Macaulay suggested a Baconian method of constructing political axioms based upon observations of past and present elementary facts of human action, "carefully combining and contrasting those which are authentic."[14] Mill reproached Macaulay for the narrowness of this outmoded and purely experimental method, asserting that Macaulay's "notions of philosophizing might have recognised Kepler, but would have excluded Newton and Laplace."[15]

The result of this criticism, however, was not a defense of his father's view. "As applicable to politics," says Mill, this geometrical style of imputing universal premises to circumstances, the effects of which are complex and multifarious, is "fundamentally erroneous."[16] "Geometry, which, not being a science of causation at all, does not require or admit of any summing-up effects."[17] It is thus clear that Mill's critique of Macaulay's and his father's methodology was not one-sided. It may be suggested that Mill's general formulations against the chemical or experimental method, as well as the geometrical or deductive method, represents a corresponding negation of Baconism on the one hand and Hobbesism and Benthamism on the other. Mill did not turn away completely from these methods nor did he provide a radical reconstruction of them; instead he combined them into a two-fold method of induction and deduction.

To be sure, this newly fashioned, or to be more precise, altered and reinforced method of observation, owes its essential formalization to Comte. As Mill concluded in his reassessment of the *Cours de philosophie positive*, Comte's method of studying social phenomena "is highly instructive" and "must be, in substance, the same as in all other sciences."[18] The method of "inverse deduction," as Comte called it, breaks down to some simple elements. First, the method employed in the physical sciences must be reversed to enable a positive social science. Whereas in the former individual facts and findings lead to conclusions about human nature, in the latter specific experiences are studied in the light of fundamental laws. Next, variations, or historically discernible deviations, are deduced from the basic laws of human nature. And although the development of knowledge cannot ignore such modifications fully, it would be rash to abandon the general tendencies observable in society for chance peculiarities. And finally, according to this method, variations that relate to general laws are tested by aggregating a large number of individual cases so as to establish a "constant quantity." Through this method, "The very events which in their own nature appear most capricious and uncertain," says Mill, can be known to us "with a degree of regularity approaching to mathematical."[19]

One of the important distinctions to be made between Comte's account of the inverse deductive method and Mill's account is that Mill put a much greater emphasis on the regularity and predictability of human occurrences. This consideration may be said to be the crowning feature of the last two books of his *Logic*; it is also Mill's primary criticism of Comte's theory in the *Cours de philosophie positive*. Mill's discussion of what Comte neglected is worth quoting at length:

Our space is not consistent with inquiry into all the limitations of this doctrine. It requires many of which M. Comte's theory takes no account. There is one, in particular, dependent on a scientific artifice familiar to students of science, especially of the application of mathematics to the study of nature. When an effect depends on several variable conditions, some of which change less, or more slowly, than others, we are often able to determine, either by reasoning or by experiment, what would be the law of variation of the effect if its changes depended only on some of the conditions, the remainder being held constant. The law so found will be sufficiently near truth for all times and places in which the latter set of conditions do not vary greatly, and will be a basis to set out from, when it becomes necessary to allow for the variations of those conditions also. Most of the conclusions of social science applicable to practical use are of this description. M. Comte's system makes no room for them.[20]

Clearly Mill believed that the social qualities of mankind, despite their various differentiations, are subject potentially to invariable laws and methods of measurement. Applied to social phenomena, Mill is suggesting that with each set of qualitative differences between individuals, there can be found certain predictable limits within which they will act. True, for Mill these universal laws of social development may not be as easily defined as chemical and physical regularities; still the intensity of psychological and social features can be observed and verified as a whole.

In the same work in which Mill questioned the validity of many of Comte's speculations, he also rallied to his defense from the attacks Herbert Spencer made upon him. Here again, Mill provides an illustration of how closely related quantification is to the activity of induction. His treatment of the matter begins with Spencer's comment in his *Genesis* that science, "while purely inductive is purely qualitative.... All quantitative prevision is reached deductively; induction can achieve only qualitative prevision."[21] Mill writes:

Now if we remember that the very first accurate quantitative law of physical phenomena ever established, the law of the accelerating force of gravity, was discovered and proved by Galileo partly at least by experiment; that the quantitative laws on which the whole theory of the celestial motions is grounded, were generalized by Kepler from direct comparison of observations; that the quantitative law of the condensation of gases by pressure, the law of Boyle and Mariotte, was arrived at by direct experiment; that the proportional quantities in which every known substance combines chemically with every other, were ascertained by innumerable experiments, from which the general law of chemical equivalents, now the ground of the most exact quantitative previsions, was an inductive generalization: we must conclude that Mr. Spencer has committed himself to a general proposition, which a very slight consideration of truths perfectly known to him would have shown to be unsustainable.[22]

Like Bacon, Mill formulated canons or rules that he recommended as the proper methods of any experimental inquiry. These rules may be conceived, as we shall see, both qualitatively and quantitatively.

The inquiry falls under the rubric of cause and effect; one can understand the connection between these two conditions through the principal method of agreement and difference. For Mill, the simplest way of determining the cause-effect connection between two events or situations is to begin by investigating all of the instances that are present and common to a given circumstance. In the method of agreement, "If two or more instances of the phenomenon under investigation have only one circumstance in common, the circumstance in which alone all the instances agree is the cause (or effect) of the given phenomenon."[23] Accordingly if we wish to ascertain the causal relation of tides, for instance, we will endeavor first to point out the presence of phenomena connected to the flow and ebb of the ocean over a successive period. We would doubtless note a great variety of particulars, such as two tides occurring every day, higher tides during certain seasons, the sun and moon, and the family cock crowing after the tides are lowest. In trying to find only the legitimate cause of, say, flowing tides, we would proceed to investigate which circumstance appears distinct from the others with regard to being the most unchanging. We eliminate, literally, the cock and find that notwithstanding its absence, the flowing phenomenon of the tides is still present. This leads us to consider the other circumstances and to determine if one of them alone is present when the phenomenon occurs.

It is hardly necessary to point out the difficulty that now arises to any conclusion that Mill's method of agreement may establish. However much we reduce the number of instances connected to a given phenomenon, we can never demonstrate a single, final cause by this operation. In the case of the flowing tides, the attraction of the sun and moon, higher tides depending on the season, and the occurrence of two tides roughly every twenty-four hours will always be present to the phenomenon at hand. This method is therefore encumbered by co-existent causes. As Mill put it, "The obscurity and difficulty of the investigation of the laws of phenomena is singularly increased by the necessity of adverting to these two circumstances, intermixture of effects and plurality of causes."[24]

Although the method of difference compares the occurrence of instances as does the previous method, it nevertheless provides an alternative mode of examination. As formulated by Mill, it states, "If an instance in which the phenomenon under investigation occurs and an instance in which it does not occur have every circumstance in common save one, that one occurring only in the former, the circumstance in which alone the two instances differ is the effect, or the cause, or an indispensable part of the cause, of the phenomenon."[25] This canon denotes the opposite of the former method, but our proceeding under its instructions would not lead us to any invariant relation either. If we continue our example of finding the causality between remarkably high tides and the attraction of the sun and moon, the inadequacy of this method becomes apparent, for the method of difference requires two relevant factors that in this particular example cannot completely be fulfilled: exactly similar situations and a single event. Only in the first instance is the method applicable; the strongest tides occur when the sun and moon (at the time of the new and full moon) act in the same direction; a cyclic phenomenon of nature and therefore determinate. But the canon does not inform us which of the two attractive forces, the sun or the moon, is greater. Again, so long as a multiplicity of causes exists, the agreement-difference method cannot assure us of getting beyond indeterminant reasoning.

This leads us to a third, more accurate method of experimental inquiry. Mill referred to it as the method of residues and considered it most important in discovering conspicuous, or unlikely, causes. The rule estimates that "subducting from any given phenomenon all the portions which, by virtue of preceding inductions, can be assigned to known causes, the remainder will be the effect of the antecedents which had been overlooked or of which the effect was as yet an unknown quantity."[26] The investigation of residues, then, claims that given a wide range of circumstances, the sum of the effects can be subtracted from the totality, and the remaining substance becomes the real cause. The same difficulty, however, arises for this method as in the former; it proceeds on the assumption that the antecedent to a residual phenomenon can be known in isolation from an indefinite number of instances. Mill recognized this inherent limitation. For him these canons were a means of eliminating, as much as possible, extrinsic or loose-fitting circumstances. The inductive process cannot provide exact solutions; it can, however, narrow the number of causes to a merely sufficient causal relation.

No other method approaches this condition of certainty as does the method of concomitant variation. The long road of inductive reasoning culminates in this method. It attempts to prove causality through a so-called statistical connection. Moreover, it appears out of the realization that the preexisting methods were irreducible for the decisive reason that they were concerned with qualitative differences—that is, affirming, denying, or modifying the presence and absence of phenomena.[27] This is, to be sure, an inexhaustible activity; the causes of a possible effect may be infinite. On a different level, however, causality can be shown to be the quantitative measure of the variation between any two phenomena. "Suppose," says Mill, "that when A changes in quantity, a also changes in quantity, and in such a manner that we can trace the numerical relation which the changes of the one bear to such changes of the other. . . . We may then, with certain precautions, safely conclude that the same numerical relation will hold within our limits of observation."[28] To take the familiar example of the tides, we know that the height of tides can be calculated by adding their collective attractions and, simultaneously, computing the distances between the sun and the earth and the moon and the earth. Thus, as Newton showed, the moon's attraction force raises the water level ten feet, whereas the sun increases it a mere two feet. This, of course, also varies depending on the moon's distance from earth. And Mill's method of concomitant variation is more tenable in this particular example than in most others. It allows us to examine the degree of variation at different periods of the year, for instance, the vernal and autumnal equinoxes. The major fault in such correlations is that although the various combinations may be able to produce significant numerical relations, they cannot be proven causally connected. While two different phenomena may modify each other concomitantly, it does not follow that the antecedent confirms the validity of the consequent. Statistical regularity, in other words, does not in itself prove the principle of causality. As Mill concluded, "Anything like a scientific use of the method of experiment in these complicated cases is, therefore, out of the question."[29]

In his article, "On the Definition of Political Economy and On the Method of Investigation Proper to It," Mill showed that the inductive method is lacking for other reasons than those outlined in the *Logic*. He quite clearly was asserting a position here diametrically opposed to Bacon's point of view. For Bacon, scientific inquiry tries to find an *experimentum crucis*, that is, a particular circumstance that excludes both contrary and relative tendencies and may thus be said to be a causal agent proper. One sees how facile necessarily absent conditions can be found in chemistry—for example, when the experiments we are performing on the union and dissolution of particles can be controlled and distinguished carefully. "Seldom," notes Mill, do we have such powers "in ethical, and scarcely ever in political science. We cannot try forms of government and systems of national policy on a diminutive scale in our laboratories, shaping our experiments as we think they may most conduce to the advancement of knowledge."[30] In other words, the intrinsic principles of these fields of inquiry are relative, and the factors that cause or help form their character cannot be integrated and reduced to solitary elements. And it is in this context that Mill turned to and consequently linked up with deductive reasoning.

We have already seen that the commonplace polarization between inductive and deductive logic is basically misleading.[31] Mill drew a similar conclusion; whenever we are inquiring into the matter of cause and effect, "there must be a direct induction as the basis of the whole, though in many particular investigations the place of induction may be supplied by a prior deduction; but the premises of this prior deduction must have been derived from induction."[32] This, however, is not the sole condition of scientific analyses. Indeed Mill's deductive method goes beyond any particular form of inductive generalization although it remains one of its essential traits throughout.

The second operation of Mill's deductive process is ratiocination:

"This is a process of calculation, in the wider sense of the term, and very often involves processes of calculation in the narrowest sense."[33] But whatever may be argued against the inductive method of concomitant variation may be applied with equal strength to deductive computations. While mathematical truths ("the science of number," as Mill called it) should not be discarded, nevertheless they cannot provide any invariable connections. Mill saw this difficulty: "What security have we that in our computation *a priori* we have taken all these [complex phenomena] into our reckoning, . . . how vain the pretense of summing up the effects of many causes, unless we know accurately the numerical law of each."[34] It is thus necessary to extend any sort of proper analysis further.

From the idea that a valid generalization depends on an inductive process and that a statistical application cannot fully exhaust all possible instances, Mill suggested a final operation to prove the efficient causal relation between two phenomena: verification.

The added dimension of verification to Mill's theory of deduction takes on a quantitative import, for his use of this specific form of analysis sharply breaks with the traditional reliance upon experience and observation as the locus of knowledge. Mill's usage is inseparably bound up with collecting repetitive instances to establish the highest probability of a causal connection. This taking account exhibits a quantitative kind of purposiveness in the sense that Mill was treating independently varying circumstances according to degrees of relevance, predictability, or resemblance. At this stage of his analysis—undertaking to distinguish how much more or how many times less one property occasions a consequent—Mill assigned quantitative relations to qualitative ones. As Mill insisted in his essay on political economy, this a posteriori "method is notwithstanding of great value in the moral sciences, namely not as a means of discovering truth, but of verifying it and reducing to the lowest point that uncertainty of every particular case."[35] Later he says, "If we desire a nearer approach to concrete truth, we can only aim at it by taking, or endeavoring to take, a greater number of individualizing circumstances into the computation."[36]

This brings us to the end of Mill's inductive-deductive mode of investigation. Indeed, after going through its particular processes in order to find what is required for a "genuine" causal condition to be fulfilled, we can see that although his method does not give us any formula to discover causality (nor was it meant to), it is nevertheless a definitive embodiment of quantitative characteristics. As Mill himself points out, "We cannot, therefore, reason respecting causation without introducing considerations of quantity and extension at every step."[37] With these major methodological distinctions in mind, we can now consider various other ways in which his thought incorporated the forms of quantity and quality.

Of Quantity and Quality

The aim of Mill's *A System of Logic* was to reconstruct the principles of logical inquiry. Mill wanted to purify logical reasoning from ambiguity, metaphorical expression, and from the short-sighted and defective analyses of the schoolmen and Aristotle himself. But it was not only a restoration of logic that Mill had in mind; he also attempted to give a foundation to logic as certain and noncontingent as mathematical propositions. Logic, Mill claimed, was not a precise science of mere persuasion that sought to express beliefs as ultimately true; rather it was a technique to arrive at precise relations coextensive with the activity of geometry. Mill said of the province of logic that it "is not the science of Belief, but the science of Proof, or Evidence."[38]

Mill began his treatise on logic by expelling the rationale of Aristotle's famous categories of substance, quantity, quality, relation, and so on. He did not abandon these classifications entirely. They are, he said, a very superficial and inadequate guide to enumerating various aspects of both subjective and objective reality. How, for instance, can feelings be specifically accounted for under any one category? Fear may be considered a state of mind (substance), or according to how great it is (quantity), or whether it is exciting or troublesome (quality), or its reference to, say, pain (relation). Mill thus found reason to doubt the efficacy of Aristotle's classification of things. And this he did on two important grounds. First, Aristotle's distinctions are noninclusive and in fact omit primary substances, such as sensations; second, it is insufficient to consider something as involving only one category because phenomena interweave and therefore can never be said to be independent in their own right. In order to grasp the precise meaning of propositions and to distinguish between proven and unproven things, it is necessary to use other descriptions and cate-gories to go beyond the Aristotelian framework of classifying things.

It is not surprising that Mill commenced his reworking of the field of logic with the subheading "Feelings, or States of Consciousness." Mill held that "everything is a feeling of which the mind is conscious; everything which it feels, or, in other words, which forms a part of its own sentient existence."[39] Hence logic, concerned with depicting the relation between mental constructs and observable things, must pro-ceed first to distinguish kinds of sensation and the object of sensation from that which causes it.

It is also clear that Mill hardly departed here from the associationist psychology emphasized in his father's *Analysis of the Phenomena of the Human Mind*. This shows itself especially in J. S. Mill's stress on the intimate connection between sensation and volition.[40] According to associationist psychology, the external world exists for our con-sciousness, but sensations or impressions are not received passively. Rather through our own movement and activity we bring forth ob-jective reality to our sentient being, which is then instrumental in shaping particular ideas. The younger Mill also saw such impulses as decisive factors in determining the outcome of our beliefs. "All which we are aware of, even in our own minds," is (in the words of James Mill) "a certain thread of consciousness; a series of feelings, that is, of sensations, thoughts, emotions, and volitions, *more or less numerous* or complicated."[41] But the importance of establishing feeling as a primary form of logical reasoning has significant implications insofar as proportionate measurements are concerned.

After the class of feelings, Mill surveyed the variety of things that we may distinguish as substances. By substance, Mill meant either body or mind; the former excites our sensations, while the latter re-ceives feelings that have become prominent to it. Here again Mill is in agreement with his father that of the external world "we know and can know absolutely nothing, except the sensations which we experi-ence from it."[42] This dichotomy appears to be a logical consequence of Mill's phenomenalist position vis-à-vis sensations. To show that a substance is either an object or a subject meant that both body and mind first must be reduced to mere impressions and then recon-structed in terms of knowable ideas associated with one another. Moreover, we can say of substances that they are external (body) or internal (mind), but beyond that our analysis must remain purely tentative. We can never extend our understanding beyond the series of events or experiences that an external object produces upon our sensations. More than this, if we wish to know why this object caused that sensation is, according to Mill, to pursue an unattainable goal.

If the world can be approached only from the point of view of our sensations, the question arises of how we distinguish between the properties of things and the sensations that seemingly caused them. Mill's answer is that substances are easily separated from attributes. He then postulates "quality," "quantity," and "relation" as the three means of penetrating the confusion that coalesces sensible features of objects with sensations themselves (such as the attribute whiteness and the sensation of perceiving color).

Whereas in preceding investigations, especially Aristotle's, quality was recognized as multiform, for Mill a quality is grounded on the sensations.[43] Beyond the outward phenomena that are ultimately resolved into sensations, there are no qualities we can ascribe to things. Indeed, according to Mill's prescription we cannot prove that there are qualities beyond phenomena or independent of us because all we know is directly connected to sense impressions. Put another way, qualities presuppose the presence of real things and a mind that perceives them. If something is a quality, it cannot subsist by itself. It is entirely dependent on sensory data, the cornerstones of any idea.

Mill's view of qualities tends to avoid the essential Lockean error about the character of experience: that sensory states can be set over against the objective realm without any direct links between them. Mill tended to see what is real and outside us and what may be called sensation as mediated with one another. Thus to speak of snow as being white means that I see the snow, and from the multitude of sensations deep within me, the sensation of white appears as an idea or visual sense data.[44]

The connection between sensory impressions and objective reality that is found in Mill's discussion of quality reappears in his treatment of quantity. The two are substrata of a single view about the world of real things and sensory states as inextricably linked together. Hence there is no distinct polarity between quality and quantity; they are both attributes and drift toward one another by forces inherent in the doctrine of psychological association. Mill says of material substances that they all "possess quantity, consist of parts which can be numbered, and in that character possess all the properties which are called properties of numbers."[45] Elsewhere he makes a similar remark: "Motions, forces, or other influences, and times are numerable quantities, and the properties of number are applicable to them as to all other things."[46] All attributes of bodies, then, may be regarded as endowed with particular quantities, which may be perceived as equal or unequal to each other. But the units of actual bodies must be determined according to some measuring rod that is able to establish a precise relation between such objects; this is a minimum requirement. To speak of things as different in respect of their quantity means that they can be indentified to a larger or lesser degree according to a construct or fundamental measure. This yardstick, in turn, must include innumerable gradations by which one object may be said to differ from another by a certain amount. This may often be a separate, arbitrary measure inapplicable to other substances; that is, not all objects are comprehended by a common measure. But the basis for considering objects in terms of their quantity is not something arbitrarily arrived at. According to Mill, quantities, like qualities, are "always grounded on a difference in the sensations which they excite . . . [they] are grounded on states of feeling or consciousness."[47]

Mill attributed great importance to expressing subject matter in degrees: how much, how fast, how irregular, and how far. He often spoke of social phenomena as differences of degree. This quantitative enumeration of things, however, arises from the fact that Mill conceived of numbers as denoting differences in sense perceptions. As he put it, "The peculiarity I contend for is only one of degree. All our ideas of sensation, of course, resemble the corresponding sensations, but they do so with very different degrees of exactness and reliability."[48] Thus the sensations involved in picking up a bar of gold differ in degree from those corresponding to our lifting a dozen such bars.

Mill's treatment of quantity and quality in respect of properties of things is evidenced in still another way as the mixing of the two concepts to represent a single sentiment. Mill does not consider quantity and quality as a genuine pair of opposites. We are able not only to envisage things as different in kind but also in degree. But we may also apprehend objects according to quantitative differences in their essence or quality. This does not represent a mishandling of the two terms nor does Mill see it as a trivial claim. He is thinking mostly in a social context as to what degree a community may advance in qualitative features like education and representation. Insofar as we are working with physical qualities that can be related to numerical series, we shall not be led astray. The mistaken idea arises, however, when quantitative distinctions are applied to nonserial qualities. Mill was wrong, I suggest, in expressing intensive qualities as conducive to questions of degree.

There remains one aspect of Mill's classification of attributes that completes the subset: relations. Mill does not plough much new territory here beyond Aristotle's comments on the notion of relatives.[49] According to Aristotelian logic, we cannot suppose that things are what they are on their own account. Thus a mountain is only in relation to something else. Further, relatives admit of a more or less. Particular objects therefore may be sharply distinguished from each other based on the observation that one contains the other. This is the so-called fundamental relation between them, although it is not always reciprocal. Just because two qualities are related does not mean that, say, the smaller can contain the larger.

Mill's analysis of relations seems written in Aristotle's shadow. It differs from Aristotle's foregoing analysis by virtue of the fact that Mill believed a relation cannot be conceptualized without reference to those sensual relationships that comprise it. To repeat what has been discussed with regard to quality and quantity, the first and fundamental aspect of any relation is that it is a product of "series of sensations of states of consciousness."[50] Relations are, to be sure, as relevant as quality and quantity are to understanding reality in respect of specific kinds of sensory states. One might think, however, that no logical operations can be carried out unless all attributes are examined. This seems right, although Mill nowhere says so explicitly. His serious condemnation of Aristotle's *Categories* for omitting a few crucial classifications would imply this, however.

The Principles Applied to Government and Politics

We are now in a position to consider Mill's use of quality and quantity in political affairs and the way in which he attempted to treat strictly qualitative features as subject to reckonings of degree. The most important cases in which these notions are used with reference to human actions are in the three essays, "On Liberty" (1859), "Representative Government," (1861) and "Utilitarianism" (1863). First, we shall distinguish Mill's considerations of citizens as made up of so many equivalent units and the centrality of this idea to his notion of democracy.

Before we set out to explore Mill's conception of representative democracy and the ways in which commensurable quantities are associated with it, let us consider briefly the Roman republic. The point I wish to call attention to is one that we often overlook, perhaps because of our own involvement in a very different form of democratic government. There are sides to democracy other than the strictly numerical rule governing present-day viewpoints: "each to count for one and nobody to count for more than one." Admittedly the frequent gibe at classical democracy that membership in the state and participatory rights were limited to a narrow class of persons is all too true. But we are concerned here only with the criteria of selecting a plebiscite to execute governmental matters, not the system of franchise itself.

The methods of choosing public officers in the past have varied widely. Being well off financially has always been an important qualification for political careers. A stable economic footing served magistrates in attaining as well as sustaining themselves in office.[51] Except in the case of property requirements, a quantitative reckoning, other qualitative values were significant in elections. Wealth and property qualifications thus were not always enough. Social prestige, family, physical strength, jurisprudence, and oratory, among others, frequently served as factors determining who shall represent the general population. As Cicero remarked, "There are only two *artes* which can place a man in the highest office—that of general and that of the good orator."[52] In either case, such criteria are markedly qualitative and remain statistically imperceptible.

Mill begins to construct his theory as a form of calculability by endowing democracy with two principles that exhibit elements of computation: equality and proportion. We have already seen how equality (an undifferentiated correspondence between equivalent units) was inconceivable for the ancient Romans, yet it is one of the most powerful common denominators in modern constitutional theory. The democratic notion of one man, one vote seeks to establish a numerical equality whereby the value of each unit is neither overweighed nor underweighed. Thus neither numerical majorities nor minorities are allowed to have unconstrained opportunity to tip the balance through possible combinations of votes. Mill, however, recognized that government composed of more or less equal parts was easier to secure theoretically than pragmatically. In order to eliminate the discrepancies that prevailed when some groups were ostensibly favored by the representative machinery, Mill recognized the need to implement and preserve a proportionate system of representation.[53] To this he says:

In a really equal democracy, every or any section would be represented, not disproportionately, but proportionately. A majority of the electors would always have a majority of the representatives; but a minority of the electors would always have a minority of the representatives. Man for man, they would be as fully represented as the majority . . . for there is not equal suffrage where every single individual does not count for as much as any other single individual in the community.[54]

Thus in order to bring about a more equal per capita determination, it was necessary, according to Mill's conception, to weigh votes as well as to count them. By introducing proportion as a condition of popular elections, the relative strength of each unit is considered vis-à-vis every other unit. And the maxim "one man, one vote" is supplanted by the principle "one man, one value."[55]

Mill's orienting representation toward a proportionate system in which weaker parties are not excluded by virtue of their smaller number can be seen in light of his well-known opposition to the electoral system, along with his attempts to reorganize it along the lines of Hare's recommendations.[56] With respect to actual mathematical anomalies, the English system of voting at that time disturbed Mill for three reasons. First, in the simple majority or plurality system, the distribution of seats in Parliament was often disproportionate to the total votes cast for the parties themselves. Hence party strengths did not necessarily mirror voters' intentions; an overwhelming number of representatives enjoyed power in spite of the fact that they commanded support from a minority of constituents. Second, even if this discrepancy between votes and seats does not occur, minority parties invariably receive a lower proportion of seats than votes. This very fact, said Mill in his *Considerations on Representative Government*, meant the domination of minority groups who were powerless before the opinions and decrees of the numerical majority. And finally, excluding the adult woman population from the right to vote (which was not achieved until 1918) clearly established the voting system as an unequal, partial one.

At best, then, it is insufficient to approach representation as a mere determination of the majority. Proportion, not numerical pluralities, must be the basis upon which representative arrangements are arrived at. The Hare system of personal representation, says Mill, could secure just such a fair distribution of votes.[57] Under this scheme electors are entitled to list their candidates in order of preference. The quota of votes a candidate needs to win in a multimember constituency is established beforehand. Once the candidate obtains the sufficient quantity of votes, his or her surplus votes are distributed to the second order of preference, and so on until the set number of quotas is reached and the available seats filled. Various consequences emerge from this type of proportional representation. Most notable is the fact that greater representation is given to minorities, while overall majorities and party tickets are dispensed with. This broadening of the franchise would affect not only the greater sphere of personal choice but also the nature of the electoral system itself. The sole basis on which it is founded is clearly mathematical, and from these numerical results can be derived the inexhaustible evaluations of the proportionate system's efficacy and practical feasibility.[58]

As distinguished from Mill's rather straightforward treatment of representation and the quantitative assumptions it involves, the function of quantity and quality in his account of happiness and good government is somewhat more muddled. In contrast with his usage of the concepts elsewhere, his *Utilitarianism* lacks any fixed meaning of the terms and is in this sense vague. Yet the formulations are there, and the extraordinary importance Mill attaches to them warrants further inspection.

Mill borrows the formula outlined in his *Utilitarianism* directly from the teachings of his father and of Bentham; according to their doctrine, the "greatest happiness for the greatest number" is the key principle upon which legislation must take its direction. Hence the practical task falls to legislators to secure social conditions that increase the sum total of individual happiness and consequently that of the political community. When the utilitarians invoked the pleasure-pain doctrine, it was meant to embrace the whole of human affairs, including moral sensibility, penal reforms, legislation in general, and personal pleasures. They all shared the conviction that the actions of society are right in proportion as they increase happiness and produce pleasure and that government should be changed when it promotes the contraries to these determinations, unhappiness and pain.

For the moment, we can ignore what the utilitarians meant with regard to questions of pleasure and pain. The practice of considering the interests of humanity exclusively in terms of utility is bound by a regard for happiness, pleasure, and so on based upon some natural scale. This suggests that pains and pleasures can be distinguished from one another and that happiness can be measured according to specific values quite independently of any arbitrary determination or emotional inclination. To speak literally of the state's activity and the private world of the individual citizen, family, and marriage strictly in terms of maximized pleasure is absurd. Mill's own view of ethical conduct, however, to some extent avoids the superficial and unsatisfactory accounts of his mentors.[59] A government constituted according to the greatest happiness doctrine, Mill argues, must take into account qualitative as well as external or quantitative differences. Mill explicitly states the interconnection between these concepts and utilitarian attitudes toward the summum bonum of government. "The ultimate end," Mill says, "is an existence exempt as far as possible in enjoyments, both in point of quantity and quality."[60] It is important to see the significance of this point, especially against the tradition of utilitarianism stretching back to Bacon in which quantity overshadowed qualitative considerations.

Mill distinguishes qualities into several entities that are interrelated. Essentially his kinds of pleasure are presented in terms of a scaled ethical elevation; some qualities are recognized as higher than others. Moral and intellectual qualities are viewed as the most important aspects of human development; talents (especially artistic) are also envisaged as superior to those activities associated with man's corporeal pleasures. The famous claim that "it is better to be a human being dissatisfied than a pig satisfied; better to be Socrates dissatisfied than a fool satisfied" well illustrates the ascendant-descendant representation of kinds of pleasure offered by Mill's scheme.[61]

This identity of types and degrees of pleasures as the characteristic hallmark of ethical theory is also taken up by Mill in his *Considerations on Representative Government*. Here again Mill conceives the best form of government as one that insists upon the numerical maximization of apparently "good" qualities. Here is an illustration of how Mill mixes the two issues:

We may consider . . . as one criterion of the goodness of a government, the degree in which it tends to increase the sum of good qualities in the governed, collectively and individually. . . . This leaves, as the other constituent element of the merit of a government, the quality of the machinery itself; that is, the degree in which it is adapted to take advantage of the amount of good qualities . . . and make them instrumental to the right purposes.[62]

From this specific assertion for a society and an ethical standard of behavior in accordance with quantitative and qualitative factors arises a series of problems that Mill does not overcome. Mill does not entirely avoid the absurd suggestion that felicity has a purely quantitative measuring rod and that sentiments and impulses can be calculated. His statement in *Utilitarianism* that arithmetical magnitudes can be applied to valuations of happiness is hardly persuasive, and it merely repeats the same point raised by his father and by Bentham.

A second problem with Mill's conceptual distinctions is that although he recognizes that qualitative factors must be brought to bear on determinations of happiness, he takes the fallacious step of judging qualities irrespective of any independent standard other than his own subjective preferences. Thus Mill points out the demerits of so-called inferior (creature) pleasures that do not belong to, say, aesthetic appreciation, but this judgment remains purely arbitrary.[63]

Finally Mill's sketch of how degrees of pleasure are to be distinguished from kinds of pleasure is somewhat implausible. As he put it,

If I am asked what I mean by difference of quality in pleasures, or what makes one pleasure more valuable than another, merely as a pleasure, except its being greater in amount, there is but one possible answer. Of two pleasures, if there be one to which all or almost all who have experience of both give a decided preference, irrespective of any feeling of moral obligation to prefer it, that is the more desirable pleasure.[64]

Thus, in connection with the question whether a sum of satisfaction is to be preferred above a kind of satisfaction, Mill appears to set up a mechanism by which a choice may be approved or renunciated. Two possibilities seem to present themselves if we allow the determinacy of happiness a public forum. First, it is imaginable that a group of judges may decide which sort of activities can be regarded as salutary and consistent with maximizing the pleasure of society as a whole. On the other hand, a public opinion poll may be welcomed as a way of ascertaining which moral incentives are worthwhile and which do not receive the support of the governed. Mill's views on the subject seem compatible with both alternative procedures. He states, "The goodness of the administration of justice is in the compound ratio of the worth of the men composing the tribunals, and the worth of the public opinion which influences or controls them."[65] But even if we admit the desirability of certain alternative modes of operation, the formal rules and conditions are much more difficult, if not impossible, to conceive, administer, or enforce: whether the quantity and quality of enjoyments can be tested and applied to actual societies and what criteria shall be used to determine the real content of pleasure and pain.

Mill placed much emphasis on the regularity and predictability of human behavior. It is perhaps this view of individual and social phenomena as ultimately predictable in principle that throws most light on his views about psychology and ethology.

The Sciences of Mind and Society

To see what Mill means by "a really positive approach to social doctrines," it is essential to examine his account of mental and physical laws as presented in the concluding book of the *System of Logic*. Since Mill was primarily concerned with establishing a "science of human nature" beyond dispute, he devoted a chapter to setting forth what this entails and in what respects it differs from investigations into other so-called exact sciences. Fortunately for Mill, the science of human nature is not viewed as wholly analogous to the physical sciences or to mathematics. The science of human thoughts, actions, and feelings, says Mill, "falls far short of the standard of exactness now realized in Astronomy."[66] This does not mean, however, that Mill accepted the belief that a science of human affairs defies calculation and is impossible to reduce to the elementary levels of physics. Mill's aim was to provide the general foundations "for predicting phenomena in the concrete" despite the fact that these are merely tendencies and thus "for the most part only approximately true."[67] According to Mill, it is not necessary to view the phenomena of human nature as invariable in order to show general characteristics that may be true in the great majority of cases. Mill's high regard for approximate generalizations is closely linked with his utilitarian ethics. As he insists; "We must remember that a degree of knowledge far short of the power of actual prediction is often of much *practical value*."[68] Thus when Mill speaks about the laws of character formation, he has in mind partly the application of these general laws to political matters such as penal sanctions and the independence of women.

To be sure, Mill does not leave open the question whether a science of human nature is possible. It needs only a proper method of inquiry and a realistic approach to the inherent difficulties in assessing human behavior. The chief distinction he draws here is that it is possible "to make predictions" about human beings "which will *almost* always be verified, and general propositions which are almost always true."[69] After these few preliminary remarks about the aims of his science of human nature, Mill turns to an analysis of its content, which includes some methodological clarifications. This is found in the chapters of book 6 concerning the laws of mind and of ethology.

Mill defends the view of his father that human judgments, ideas, and volitions result from sensations and have to be understood by reference to them. Accordingly the phenomena of the mind are a product of an interaction between the internal and external world. Such knowledge of the causes of human consciousness has further consequences too. The most important of these is the fact "that there exist uniformities of succession among states of mind," which involves the relations or associations between ideas as such.[70] This presumably means that the development of ideas is a process that is determinable precisely. The subject matter of psychology, Mill declares, is concerned with the apparent uniformities and interrelations between mental phenomena:

between an idea a and an idea b and their unity, $a + b$. But this is not a oneness, as psychological associationists have maintained. Ideas a and b remain separate in themselves and independent of the arrangement $a + b$.

In stressing the importance of uniformities, Mill is careful to add that these states of consciousness can be studied only by experiment and direct observation. To see more clearly why Mill fashioned psychology as an appendage of experimental inquiry, we may consider his approach here vis-à-vis Comte's. According to Comte, all social phenomena are necessarily dependent on the physiological laws of individuals. Society, in Comte's sense, is comprised of elements and tissues that can be decomposed or analyzed anatomically. The social body and the individual are therefore mutually connected. A disturbance in the former is coextensive with a disease in the individual. Mill considers Comte's endeavor to establish social science based on physiological questions as disastrous and essentially misleading. His argument is that although physical conditions may influence states of consciousness, it is superfluous to regard them as laws in their own right. In other words, the scope and nature of mental activity is not entirely comformable to merely nervous muscular activity. Physiology and biology together are not enough to explain the welter of particulars that make up mental states. In short, digestion, breathing, circulation of the blood, and so forth do not constitute exclusively the subject matter of the intellectual world. Indeed, says Mill, memory, intuition, and associative images ultimately may be connected to sensuousness, but these are not immediately governed by alternating conditions in the outer world.

A main feature of psychology, then, rests on the method of inquiring into human judgments and desires. For Mill, this must be carried out by means of observation and experimentation. But Mill draws attention to the fact that psychology has other important characteristics, such as determining the different degrees of intensity of volitions and feelings. It is true, says Mill, "that different minds are susceptible in very different degrees to the action of the same psychological causes."[71] His point here is that the nature of mental phenomena is essentially quantitative. In other words, the root of all relations between mental peculiarities and sense data is quantity. This view is not strictly limited to the scope of psychology as shown earlier.

Nevertheless, Mill's use of the doctrine here well illustrates its central position in his thought.

When discussing how degrees of intensity most clearly express mental differences, Mill notes the significance of quantitative features on qualities. This is especially true in psychology where "different *qualities* of mind, different types of mental character, will naturally be produced by mere differences of intensity in the sensations generally."[72] Changes in the intensity of sensations can alter a state of consciousness radically. This is most apparently seen in cases of physical torture. The essentially quantitative character of psychological inquiries, however, is evident at once. This is also a predominant feature of Mill's attempt to give a scientific form to the study of ethology.

Ethology, Mill says, "may be called the Exact Science of Human Nature."[73] This does not mean that it admits of the same certainty and precision as, for instance, determinations of the lengths of curves or of centers of mass. Rather it is the study of character development, which affirms only tendencies, not facts.

At first glance, it is hard to see what Mill means by character formation. So far, he has dealt with the individual and pointed out that the amount of sensory input an individual receives has an immanent consequence on his psychological nature. Ethology is the sum or average of the different thoughts and feelings of individuals within a society. People act and feel in different ways, but these variations can be enumerated in a mathematical fashion. And it is possible to infer the thoughts and feelings of persons in a given circumstance if the particularity of the situation is roughly repeated and if the type of behavior or attitude is statistically formulated. Mill put it this way:

It is possible to determine what makes one person, in a given position, feel or act in one way, another in another; how any given mode of feeling and conduct, compatible with the general laws (physical and mental) of human nature, has been, or may be, formed. In other words, mankind have not one universal character, but there exist universal laws of the Formation of Character.[74]

The difficult task Mill is faced with is ascertaining the real character or qualities of a given collective body. What ethology has to do with mathematical determinations becomes readily apparent here.

Character evaluations, argues Mill, can be grasped only by finding out the "marked mental qualities or deficiencies [which] *oftenest* exist."[75] Determinations of this kind are a product of simple numerical notation. Mill provides no other rules by which the results of a national character appraisal can be derived. The differences that can be seen to exist between nations are "not . . . of kinds, but of ratios and degrees."[76]

Nevertheless Mill did lay down principles for testing the results of his inquiry and for avoiding hasty generalizations. This, too, is a purely mathematical exposition. According to Mill, the validity of character determinations is proved by means of computing a large number of instances in order to diminish chance formations. This method rests on the assumptions that a proof can be given based on the quantity of cases that satisfy certain conditions. "Since in proportion as the differences are slight," adds Mill, this method of verification "requires a greater number of instances to eliminate chance."[77]

It may be said that the science of ethology enters mathematical territory inasmuch as it deduces the properties of a nation from a statistical average and then attempts to confirm its conclusions by collecting a significant number of instances that express the characteristic under investigation.

One cannot leave the subject of ethology without noticing that as a science it has made little advance since the time of Mill.[78] So far as the credit of inventing the science of ethology can be put down to any one person, we may perhaps also assign its rapid fall into oblivion to Mill. Mill's interests in the field of inquiry began to wane between his *System of Logic* (1843) and *Principles of Political Economy* (1848). After 1850, when the third edition of the *System of Logic* was published, Mill turned to subjects of more practical and public interest. Also because ethology was so difficult to establish as a science, Mill left it for the less indeterminate formulas and definitions of political economy. Mill perhaps realized that ethology contains infinite variables and problems in applying particular numerical conditions to high-order generalities and with it a firmer science than that based on bald premises.

Notes

1. John Stuart Mill, *Autobiography* (London, 1873), p. 6.

2. Ibid. The textbook referred to is Jeremiah Joyces's *Scientific Dialogues* (London, 1809).

3. Mill, *Autobiography*, pp. 30–31.

4. Mill, *A System of Logic* (London, 1941), p. 545 (hereafter referred to as *Logic*). See also his *Spirit of the Age* (1831) (Chicago, 1942), p. 1, where Mill distinguishes between "men of present age, and the men of the past."

5. For Mill's indebtedness to Comte, see his *Autobiography*, pp. 210, 245fn; *Lettres inedites de John Stuart Mill a Auguste Comte avec les responses de Comte* (Paris, 1899), pp. 2–10. See also I. W. Mueller, *John Stuart Mill and French Thought* (Urbana, Illinois, 1956), chap. 4.

6. Mill, *Autobiography*, p. 165.

7. "Bacon's conception of scientific inquiry had done its work," said Mill, "science has now advanced into a higher stage." *Logic*, p. 578.

8. Letter to Theodor Gomperz, August 19, 1854, in Heinrich Gomperz, *Theodor Gomperz, 1832–1912* (Vienna, n.d.) vol. I, p. 178.

9. Mill, *Logic*, p. 149.

10. Cf. F. J. Murray, "Mathematics and the Exact Sciences," *Philosophia Mathematica* 10 (Winter 1973): 134–54.

11. Mill, preface to the first edition, *Logic*, p. 5.

12. Ibid., p. 7.

13. Mill, *Autobiography*, p. 157. See Thomas B. Macaulay, "Mill's Essay on Government," *Edinburgh Review* 49 (March 1829): 328–67.

14. Macaulay, "Mill's Essay," p. 366.

15. Mill, *Autobiography*.

16. Ibid., p. 158.

17. Ibid., pp. 160–61. See also Mill, *Logic*, book 6, chap. 8.

18. Mill, *August Comte and Positivism* (London, 1908), p. 83.

19. Mill, *Logic*, p. 608.

20. Mill, *Comte and Positivism*, p. 88.

21. Herbert Spencer, "The Genesis of Gaseous Nebulae," appendix D in *First Principles*, 6th ed. (London, 1928). See also his *Reasons for dissenting from the Philosophy of M. Comte* (London, 1884).

22. Mill, *Comte and Positivism*, p. 46n.

23. Mill, *Logic*, p. 255.

24. Ibid., p. 286.

25. Ibid., p. 256.

26. Ibid., p. 264.

27. Cf. Morris Cohen and Ernest Nagel, *An Introduction to Logic and Scientific Method* (London, 1939), p. 152.

28. Mill, *Logic*, p. 264.

29. Ibid., p. 299.

30. Mill, *Logic*, ed. Ernest Nagel (New York, 1950), pp. 426–27.

31. See Sir J. Herschel, *A Preliminary Discourse on the Study of Natural Philosophy* (London), 1831, p. 181. "The inductive and deductive methods of inquiry may be said to go hand in hand, the one verifying the conclusions deduced by the other; and the combination of experiment and theory . . . forms an engine of discovery infinitely more powerful than either taken separately."

32. Mill, *Logic*, p. 299.

33. Ibid., p. 300.

34. Ibid., p. 303.

35. Mill, *Logic*, ed. Nagel, p. 431.

36. Mill, *Logic*, p. 587.

37. Ibid., p. 406.

38. Mill, *Logic*, ed. Nagel, p. 5.

39. Ibid., p. 32.

40. See Mill, *Autobiography*, p. 136. See also Alexander Bain, *The Senses and the Intellect* (London, 1855), and *The Emotions and the Will* (London, 1859). Bain was a collaborator of J. S. Mill.

41. Mill, *Logic*, p. 40. Emphasis added.

42. Ibid., p. 39.

43. See Aristotle, *Categories*, in *The Works of Aristotle*, ed. W. D. Ross (Oxford, 1928), 8b25ff.

44. See Mill, *Logic*, p. 43.

45. Ibid., p. 167.

46. Ibid., p. 212.

47. Ibid., p. 46.

48. Ibid., p. 155.

49. Compare Aristotle, *Categories*, 6a36.

50. Mill, *Logic*, p. 47.

51. The Roman citizenry, for example, was divided into six classes based on capital worth ranging from the first or upper class possessing 100,000 *asses* or more, down to the lowest class, called the *proletari*, with a capital worth of under 11,000 *asses*. It was an unknown practice for the relatively impoverished classes to seek political office. See Livy, *History of Rome*, I, xlii–lxii, quoted in Naptali Lewis and Meyer Reinhold, *Roman Civilization* (New York, 1951), vol. 1, p. 94. For the emergence of technical expertise as a basis of selection, see Max Weber, *Economy and Society*, ed. Guenther Roth and Claus Wittich (New York, 1968), vol. 3, chap. 11.

52. Quoted in T. P. Wiseman, *New Men in the Roman Senate* (Oxford, 1971), p. 118.

53. Not until 1944 in England were there any permanent commissions set up to determine an electoral quota by the size of constituencies. Hitherto some larger constituencies were roughly thirty-five times that of the smallest constituencies.

54. Mill, "Considerations on Representative Government," in *Three Essays* (Oxford, 1975), pp. 248–49.

55. "One man, one value." Even this requirement can lead to substantial inequalities, as witnessed by Mill's own support of plural voting in which bankers, merchants, manufacturers, foremen, and university graduates were given additional rights by virtue of their "mental superiority." See ibid. The system of plural voting was abolished in 1948.

56. See Mill, *Autobiography*, pp. 258ff.

57. See Thomas Hare, *Treatise on the Election of Representatives* (London, 1859).

58. See William H. Riker and Lloyd S. Shapley, "Weighted Voting: A Mathematical Analysis for Instrumental Judgements," and Robert Nozick, "Weighted Voting and 'One-Man, One-Vote,' " in *Representation*, ed. J. Rolland Pennock and John W. Chapman (New York, 1968).

59. "To some extent." In an important passage Mill positively asserts the sanctioning authority of quantity in the basic character of human and physical nature: "The truths of arithmetic are applicable to the valuation of happiness, as of all other measurable quantities," *Utilitarianism*, ed. Oskar Piest (New York, 1957), p. 77. Mill leaves little doubt here about the significance of quantity in conceiving science, politics, and ethics.

60. Ibid., p. 16. See also *Three Essays*, p. 153.

61. Mill, *Utilitarianism*, p. 14.

62. Mill, "On Liberty," in *Three Essays*, p. 168.

63. Cf. Maurice Cranston, *John Stuart Mill* (London, 1968), p. 12.

64. Mill, *Utilitarianism*, p. 12.

65. Mill, *Three Essays*, p. 168.

66. Mill, *Logic*, p. 553.

67. Ibid., p. 554.

68. Ibid., p. 567. Emphasis added.

69. Ibid., p. 554.

70. Ibid., p. 556.

71. Ibid., p. 559.

72. Ibid., p. 560.

73. Ibid., p. 567.

74. Ibid., p. 564.

75. Ibid., p. 565.

76. Ibid., p. 566.

77. Ibid.

78. Particular formulations using cross-national data, however, are still to be found. See, for example, Margaret Mead, "The Study of National Character," in *The Policy Sciences*, ed. Daniel Lerner and Harold D. Lasswell (Stanford, California, 1951).

(5)

Conclusion and Commentary

> It is quality rather than quantity that matters.
> —*Epistles*
> There are no numbers and no statistics in the theory of constitutions.
> —*Bagehot*

This analysis of Bacon, Hobbes, and Mill points to an unalterable penchant toward quantity and quantitative understanding at the expense of qualitative considerations. Despite the differences in their recommendations, ideas, and factual material of analysis, a particular, albeit concordant, continuity is arrived at. A rigid insistence upon the extant state of the mathematico-physical sciences accounts, to a large extent, for this common theme running through their works.

The preceding chapters showed the role and influence of quantity in their vast philosophical efforts. The object of this chapter is to summarize this reverence for quantitative perspectives and to show briefly how they and other writers who related quantity and quality by way of distinction are the lineal progenitors of the underlying faith in quantification found in modern political scientists. Finally, I present a criticism of formulating political propositions in terms of quantity, along with a discussion of how a more qualitative understanding can be realized.

Bacon extolled the sensible or corporeal world and estimated highly the materialist philosophies of the Greeks, especially that of Democritus. But he was aware that the simple reduction of phenomena to sensible entities was hardly ground enough for accurate, scientific knowledge. What was required instead was vigorous experimentation based upon experience, induction, and calibrated instrument. His method—needlessly overfactual and turgid—is applicable, he asserted, to politics, logic, morals, and the natural sciences alike. Bacon seemed to be quite unaware of the shortcomings of such an undifferentiated methodology, probably because of his great desire to render knowledge in general as strikingly evident and absolute as possible.

Thus it is relatively easy to comprehend Bacon's overvaluation of science and mathematics, then regarded as the most infallible and exact forms of understanding. He also considered them the best agents to realize unconditional certainty—hence his important maxim that the most promising and effective studies of nature "begin with physics and end in mathematics."

The root of this basic adherence to mathematico-physical reasoning lies in the unambiguous and pragmatically important value of quantity. For Bacon quantity was the *specificatum*, the ultimate determination of nature and natural philosophy. Quantification was contemplated by Bacon in his advocating that material bodies and referential virtues be "numbered, weighed, measured, defined. . . ." And although Bacon himself never sought to mathematize his suppositions, this idea that quantifications and rules of measure led to philosophical certainty served as the veritable foundation for the bulk of his works.

Like Bacon, Hobbes rejected the simple and often uniform truths derived from sense data. Hobbes, however, believed that knowledge and truth are obtained through calculation, an assumption that Bacon would be reluctant to accept. This procedure is heavily loaded with quantitative elements, but it provides the potential safeguard that all of the propositions will be deduced in a more systematic way than Bacon's procedure. Unfortunately Hobbes's system is not pure logico-mathematical reasoning, for in addition to this geometric aspect is the mechanical or physical cognition of the nature of things. And explicitly or implicitly, Hobbes reemphasized the Baconian credo concerning bodies and virtues as ultimately determined by quantities. Thus, according to Hobbes, anything that cannot be measured or accounted to be so much is suprarational and unaccessible to our rational faculties.

To this way of cognition, says Hobbes, belong architecture, navigation, astronomy, physics, politics, and moral philosophy, among others. This odd assortment reminds us of Bacon's all-embracing theoretical constructs, but we were principally concerned with the relation of this form of reasoning to political and social conduct. Taken to this narrow limit, we can discern in Hobbes's writings a strong quantitative current, indicated by the use that he made of the seemingly universal and invariable "general inclination of mankind," which he says is "a perpetual and restless striving of power after power, that ceaseth only in death." From this Hobbes deduced the common denominator of man's behavior: the maximization of individual appetites coupled with the effective minimization of chance of death or coercion against one's will. And inasmuch as all men are equal, they differ only in terms of tangible, extraneous degrees. By this Hobbes meant that their differences depend in comparative magnitudes on the ways each builds up and asserts his wishes upon another. We are all master calculators, according to Hobbes; some, however, do their "sums" comparably better than others.

Hobbes's inflated use of the arithmetical procedure resulted in the application of preestablished rules to govern commonwealths. These laws are without any distinction of type because they are naturally given and thus supposedly inviolable by subsequent political systems. What this means is that, like geometry, civil society is governed by certain preestablished axioms, regardless of historic periods. Political processes are thus governed by dominant patterns or principles rather than cycles, oscillations, and irregularities. Finally, the same quantitative traits ascribed by Hobbes to individual behavior function at a higher level with respect to existing forms of justice. Both distributive and commutative justice—the one concerned with the collective allotment of goods, rights, facilities, and benefits, the other with the exchange and competition for raw materials, finished products, and so forth between contracting parties—are products of mathematical theory. They diverge from one another only in the sense that distributive justice shifts values proportionately, whereas commutative justice values are spread either equally or unequally. More precisely, commutative justice means that the best-sellers in the market-place are the most effective arithmeticians. But taken as a whole, justice for Hobbes is predominantly a matter of increasing a quantity of value or minimizing one's potential losses.

When two seemingly one-sided approaches meet, their exaggerated elements are likely to transform or diffuse into somewhat more congenial factors. Such is the case with Mill, who, while in the process of criticizing the general formulations of Bacon and Hobbes, among others, developed a somewhat different methodology, which he (and Comte) called inverse deduction. This approach essentially fused the lagging and uninventive inductive process with the invariable and universal tendencies prevalent to deduction. Uniformities of different social phenomena are first observed everywhere, argues Mill, and then their behavioral or material forms are verified according to their statistical significance. Investigations that seek to establish a significant probability of causal connectedness, "introducing considerations of quantity . . . at every step," are far more sound and precise than all previous philosophies and systems of cognition.

We have also seen how Mill, while approving observational, inverse deduction, and quantitative methods of studying political phenomena, integrated these into his own political doctrines. This is evident first in his sharp criticisms of the nineteenth-century electoral system in England and, consequently, in his (and Hare's) recommendations to institute a proportional system of representation. This would have meant greater representation for minorities who were subjected to the incessant dominance of the few major political parties.

In addition, this preeminence of quantitative dimensions is applied by Mill to the whole of mankind in his social-philosophic brand of utilitarianism. And despite his realization that the "greatest happiness principle" assumes a quantitative as well as a qualitative character, still first and foremost is the arithmetic measuring rod by which valuations of felicity are determined. To this, other similar logical criticisms of Mill's doctrine set forth in *Utilitarianism* were added. Principal among these was the lack of any meaningful way in which he suggested that degrees of pleasure can be distinguished from kinds of pleasure. His position in regard to this question does not preclude a tribunal of judges or even an opinion poll that would publicly determine happiness. Even from a purely pragmatic standpoint, this position is highly untenable.

The final instance of Mill's prescription of how to ground scientific exactness into social and political theory concerns ethology, which Mill called the "Exact Science of Human Nature." Ethology embraces the thoughts, feelings, behavior, and character of a whole society. These properties can be turned into statistical averages, says Mill, and then compared with those of other countries. Whatever the shortcomings of this subject were, it is important to see how stamped it was by a faith in statistical formulations. Discovery and formulation of character determinations involves observing particular thoughts, feelings, and so forth that steadily repeat themselves. The guiding factor is the number of times these characteristics occur within a given population, and the principle for designating certain types of conduct as "laws of human behavior" or "laws of sociopolitical development" is the greater number of times it is realized in the course of time. For Mill, then, verification consisted of a progressive arithmetic unfolding. Because of Mill's increasing decline of interest in ethology and the logical and factual problems inherent to the study, endeavors into such preoccupations subsided instead of intensifying.

The discussion of Bacon, Hobbes, and Mill was intended to depict the trend to quantification, a trend which has had a powerful effect on the entire development of modern political knowledge. This way of looking at the objects of political inquiry—as given quantities and calculable configurations—taken so often for granted in North America, would have much surprised Aristotle, for whom the art of politics could be looked at only in terms of excess and defect. It would have surprised still more Hegel who warned of the prejudices involved in asking "how much" questions at the expense of "what kind" questions.

This cult of quantity was fostered by the deference many great thinkers paid to the natural sciences and to mathematics. The imitation of past ideals by twentieth-century political writers is also readily recognizable. Largely cultivated in isolated university departments, this has become an integral part of governmental research and development. A thrust of great significance in this long-run movement appeared during the formative years of the American political science profession between about 1900 and 1945.

John Burgess, for example, claimed in his *Political Science and Comparative Constitutional Law* (1896) that there could be objective description and precise measurement of politics and jurisprudence if the method of inquiry "which has been found so productive in the domain of Natural Science were utilized."[1] And William Munro made the following interesting observation in his *The Invisible Government* (1927):

There must be laws of politics, for laws are the most universal of all phenomena. Everything in nature inclines to move in seasons, or in undulations, or in cycles . . . . prosperity and depression, conservatism and radicalism, courage and caution, follow each other with fairly measurable regularity. We see the more or less regular sequence of revolution, reaction, normalcy, liberalism, radicalism; and then revolution again—the cycle completed.[2]

At the same time that modern political scientists were restating an admiration for the natural sciences and an ability to interpret human behavior precisely in terms of amounts, there were those with a practical bent who gave much attention to using quantitative material in governmental decision making. Thus Albert Shaw, in his presidential address before the third annual meeting of the American Political Science Association (1907), urged scientific studies of political life, "with a view to the orderly presentation of facts and the formulating of conclusions that will be of practical benefit to the perplexed legislator."[3] And Jesse Macy, in a similar address a decade later, claimed, "Science and democracy have come into the modern world at the same time. They are mutually related as cause and effect."[4]

Charles Merriam, perhaps above all others, pushed scientific politics into the processes of "social and political control." As he stated in his *New Aspects of Politics* (1925), "The close observation of governmental experiments, the prompt interchange of experience, the thoughtful consideration of the data assembled, will go far toward the wise management of public affairs."[5] Like others, centuries before him, Merriam argued that political understanding was lagging considerably behind the triumphs obtained in quantifying and interpreting the laws of the physical universe.

G. E. G. Catlin, in his *The Science and Method of Politics* (1927), set out to fill that supposed time gap and to establish once and for all a degree of political "scientificness." Magnitudes could be attached most readily to the vote, Catlin believed, which served as a yardstick for measuring "power." In this sense, politics truly may be considered "a science of prediction," according to Catlin.[6]

In the same year, 1927, an overwhelmingly optimistic report appeared by a leading social scientist, who declared that soon "it will be possible for political scientists to cease considering their field as one of formal description and legalistic philosophy, and regard it as a *natural science.* And furthermore, when so regarded, political science and behavioristic psychology become one and the same thing."[7]

Granted that this picture is somewhat oversimplified—succeeding years have brought to fruition several even more scientific studies—one may wonder whether modern political science could boast of deepening our insights or of sharpening our vision of political phenomena.[8] It is certainly beyond question that now we can amass more data and empirical regularities in support of particular policies than could, say, William Petty. In the discipline of politics, however, this throws less light on the way things are (qualitatively speaking) than the way statistics shows us they have to be, despite the many conflicting and opposite positions that are too often simply rejected as deviations.

It is an implicit judgment of this work that modern studies involving quantification, culminating in the area of public opinion prediction by Gallup and others, have only faintly advanced—in some cases to the point of absurdity—devices and processes known beforehand.[9] This, however, will likely remain an unresolved dispute between those who seek high degrees of quantitative accuracy in political analyses and those who place their efforts in developing qualitative methods.

Objections to quantitative discourse and positive methodology were raised early by writers in the fields of literature and aesthetics. Butler, Goethe, Keats, Wordsworth, Lamb, and Shelley, among others, all set about to detach their forms of discourse from the mathematizing habit.[10] Despite some recent discussions aimed at reconstructing basic premises in political philosophy, there has not occurred any significant reversal of this trend.[11]

In these concluding remarks, therefore, I sketch a view of political understanding that will avoid positivistic tendencies and overcome the preoccupations of mathematical model building. My view is neither a complete nor a step-by-step solution to methodological controversies; all that I hope to provide is an indication of a qualitative descriptive technique whereby the elementary building blocks of politics can be analyzed.

The Adequacy of Political Knowledge

It is clear that as a preliminary to any understanding of political experience, it is necessary that the concepts or fundamental terms used in such cognition be explained. These general principles indicate the content of political activity and reveal the distinctiveness of its subject matter. On this view, the notions cannot be substituted for experience, and yet the essential meaning of political activity cannot be grasped except in and through the notions. Inasmuch as the principal terms of political theory presuppose and are entailed in concrete political activity, they are not mere reference points, formulas, or decrees as commonly suggested. Nor are the notions miscellaneous and floating in the air. They are inside experience, moments and remembrances of particular political activity. Political inquiry, then, may be described as consisting of distinctions, determinations, and identifications of the specific subject matter of politics. Its ultimate object is not the accumulation of facts, a search for infallible proofs, self-evident principles, or standardizable activities; rather it is an experience and activity of making political matters intelligible. Although the concepts of politics exhibit and lay bare the content of political activity, they are not coordinate with the particular context or facts of a certain political experience. An irresponsible use of power by the executive, for instance, is not equivalent to power in general. Were this so, the diverse meaning of the concept itself would be permanently fixed and exhausted.

Nevertheless, there are specific, identifiable forms in which the conceptual postulates of political experience most distinctly appear and are most visibly and substantially realized. Any study that attempts to come to grips with the nature of political phenomena therefore presupposes a political actuality, conditions that are characteristic of political relations, and facts, ideas, and expressions about political reality. To use a well-known statement by Hegel in his introduction to the *Philosophy of Right*, "The shapes which the concept assumes in the course of its actualization are indispensable for the knowledge of the concept itself."[12]

The specific character of the term *international*, for example, was vague and raw to seventeenth-century Europe. Bentham (as late as 1780), in his *Principles of Legislation*, noted its embryonic form: "The word *International*, it must be acknowledged, is a new one....

It is calculated to express . . . the branch of law which goes commonly under the name of the *law of nations*."[13] Its so-called shape, however, became more complex and operative with the establishment of the International Working Men's Association in 1864, which, as a federation of socialist parties and organizations, pitted itself against the existing legal associations. And it is useful here to recall another instance of the term before it gained widespread acceptance: the journal entitled *Internationale*, edited by Rosa Luxemburg and Franz Mehring, which first appeared in 1915. Hence to speak of the development of political thought means that some notions become more fully realized than preceding notions; some are more adequate than others, some become exhausted, most get altered, and new ones filter into political discourse as well. Their meaning is determined in being cashed or used in the elucidation of either a past political experience—that is why the terms are considered remembrances (or "Notes" as Hobbes called them)—or in relation to a political phenomenon of current interest.

Having considered political knowledge as a reconstruction of political experience, now we can move on to a further analysis of our preliminary focus of attention: the view that the notions of politics are essentially qualitative and that quantitative conceptions of them cannot begin to tap their meaning and significance. At a higher level than the discipline of politics, it would seem that this conclusion enhances our understanding of the immense gulf between qualitative and quantitative determinations and their applicability to the social and the natural sciences, respectively.

The primary distinction made when we speak of a quality is that it contains characteristics essential to its nature. Now the essence of a quality is something that *is* in virtue of itself; that is, a quality has a constituent character that may be regarded as independent of alien attributes. In Aristotle's language, this is the difference between "qualities" and "qualifiers."[14] A quality may thus be said to be identical with being itself. Accordingly it would be wrong to say that it is its attributes or properties. A thing, for instance, may have this or that property that may refer to it but yet is not the thing itself. For example, *red* brick, *good* health, and *in*justice, are all references to particular objects. Were these qualifiers removed, the thing itself would not change its quality.

In a fundamental way, quantities may be said to resemble qualifiers, for quantities are aggregate units unrelated to the essential character of qualities as such. They are definite as to amounts and ultimately have only an outward form. *Five* horses, *three* parts oxide, and *bi*cycle are examples of objects expressed in terms of arithmetical values. Were these quantitative determinations removed, the types or kinds of objects would still have a significance and essential content of their own. Similarly the statement that "democratic states must have two-party or multiparty election contests" is not logically bound up with the notion of democracy, which it qualifies. Again, one of the distinguishing features of a quality is that particular qualifications applied or attached to it—in the case above, empirically demonstrated multiparties—are not fundamental (constituent) parts of the notion itself.

What is too often ignored today, and what undoubtedly remains one of Aristotle's significant claims, is that a quantitative description does not allow itself to be understood in the context of its contrary. This is of fundamental importance and is a distinction that enriches the extreme contrast between qualitative and quantitative investigations. When we assign a definite quantum to a particular entity, we identify a precise and exact amount. Thus a quantity consists of an unprovisional character, pure and simple. It completely disregards relative determinations or relations of contrariety. Qualities, on the other hand, are distinguishable by reference to opposites, which make them more explicit determinations while allowing for differences—for example, wealth and poverty, coaction and coercion, opinion and fact, and collectivism and individualism. Qualitative studies are usually concerned with the connectedness between these differents, the nature of their corelativity, and how actual political practices express such differences. We shall consider in more detail below relations of contrariety with reference to the various ways of analyzing concepts. A qualitative approach, however, is as applicable in the case of contrarieties as it is in comparisons between different objects that have within themselves a more-or-less relation. For instance, we may claim that this table is larger than that chair or that this welfare policy is more just than another policy that may be said to be less just. These, of course, also illustrate relative expressions, which are completely cut off from any equal or unequal kinds of determinants. On this analysis, then, it can be said that qualitative determinations always remain boldly conditional. They can never be applied unequivocally, calculated once and for all, increased by addition or decreased by subtraction.

Qualitative Treatment of Concepts

Next we must concern ourselves with political theorizing as an enterprise that possesses a specific form and content. It may be said that a theoretical understanding of politics can be understood apart from mathematical, physical, or psychological formulations that we foreswear from the outset, for political knowledge is concerned with identifying, delimiting, and explaining the particular activities, principles, and conditionality of public pursuits.

With little effort, one can list haphazardly much of the conceptual equipment of the language system associated with politics, such as: representation, totalitarianism, centralization, power, reification, emancipation, conservatism, class consciousness, distributive justice, enfranchisement, authority, nationalism, conflict, exploitation, praxis, democracy, sovereignty, ideology, equality, estrangement, and so forth. These terms used to designate the subject matter of political activity constitute a vast conceptual substructure. They themselves do not produce any worldly events or deeds. In order not to become dead letters, they depend upon use (as Wittgenstein insisted) and consumption, which entails recognition and specification through practical application. How then, are we to make sense of this heap of concepts? This is our primary concern now. Also we want to inquire into the analytical tools that we can rely upon to arrive at uncircumstantial understanding and yet avoid the current fashion that searches for behavioral and mathematical model building.[15]

What we are looking for is a set of theoretical conditions that will pinpoint adequately and disclose the substantive character of these abstract, general notions. Accordingly, it is helpful to regard them with respect to their *identity*, *difference*, and *corelatedness*.

At the earliest stage of grasping the manifold forms and meanings of the concepts that lay bare the content of political experience, we consider them as abstract or formal identities. This amounts to saying that each concept first emerges as an ideal character that purports to be a self-relation. At first glance, the concept displays a character that is independent, isolated, and detached. It is, to be sure, different from other concepts. But logically speaking, this difference is not yet manifest. The concept at first simply stands alone. It is merely named. It may, indeed, possess various properties but these are external to it. (Properties are also external in the sense that they may attach themselves to various other concepts—for example, the "right to strike" with respect to either "political power" or "class consciousness.") At this initial stage in the inquiry, however, the concept is without reference to other kinds of concepts. What is important is that the concept *is*, but, as such, reveals only a partial reality.

The realm of identification entails, among other things, the ways in which a concept is articulated in society through conduct, practices, customs, regulations, or common interests; its etymological origins; how it was embodied in political institutions in the past; and its relation to nonpolitical contexts (such as representation, which is used in matters concerning government, art, and literature). From this initial presentation, the meaning of the concept gradually can become more concrete and accurately formulated. At this first stage, then, we seek to examine a concept from the viewpoint of identity, mere immediacy.

For theoretical understanding, however, what is sought is more than identification. This activity discloses a missing vital element in determining the explicit content of the concept itself. We come to recognize that the concept has manifold complexities and that it is only partially understood from the angle of identification. In other words, we find our first assumption (that the content of the notion was clearly distinct) confining although not entirely profitless. This leads us to a further stage, that of difference. And if momentarily we hold the evaluations of identity in abeyance, we come to conceive the concept in terms of other notions. These stand outside the concept as an essentially formalistic other. It is here that we recognize diversity in its most naked sense. In difference, the various concepts, as others, flourish in their own characteristics but as mediated and dependent upon others, unlike the independence postulated in the stage of identity. To understand a term in its difference is to acknowledge contingent relations, loose connections, and varieties of nuances. It is, perhaps, analogous to finding oneself in an orchard where all of the fruit at first appears similarly ripened. The concepts in political macrotheory exhibit this very multiplicity of qualities or *differentia*, each separate from the others.

But it is also true that as differents the concepts are unique and express an abstract truth of their own, as differents at the same moment they are externally related to others. The characteristics of difference are seldom found in combination; their conditionality can be expressed either as variety or comparison. Variety entails an immediate and widespread view of the concepts, appearing in any number of shapes. It refers to the mere diversity of the concepts that at this moment appear disconnected and miscellaneously expressed. Except as appearing as political topics, the relationships remain loose and indefinite.

It is also here, however, that difference entails actual similarities with and differences from other qualities. Accordingly a comparative relation issues forth, and it is found after close investigation that some concepts are principally concerned with others, treat some acts in a like manner, and guard their territorial borders in other instances. Aristotle was a pioneer in laying the intellectual foundation for the comparative approach in politics. This was based, however, on his underlying principle that "it is in the virtue of qualities only that things are called similar or dissimilar" and can thus be compared with each other.[16] Inasmuch as this is a major sphere of political understanding, and also the most easily trampled upon, it deserves further comment.

In comparative analyses, similarities of different things and differences in similar things are sought. In political texts, for example, power and authority are different yet in many instances treated alike.[17] Comparative analyses of government systems continually encounter common likenesses in countries with unlike institutions and unlike social and cultural factors.[18] The difficulties arise, however, in trying to determine for what reasons the differents may be regarded as alike and at what point another notion is unrelated to the individual different. It is clear that whoever strays far away in attempting to tailor terms to fit specific purposes ends up drawing absurdities and whoever steps meekly between terms is likely to be blamed for using them synonymously. Just how far it is possible to stray without reaching either extreme cannot be treated arithmetically. In practice, it is something variable that, with the utmost care and precision, cannot be delimited and empirically verified.

What is clear, however, is that of all the potential relations between fundamental terms, the regulative principle that most directly captures their meaning is that of contrariety. Corelated distinctions of this kind are extremely significant for embracing the interrelations among these variations and for approaching qualitative problems as a whole. We have already seen that as a formal identity, the concept is particular and not as yet developed explicitly. In difference the concepts enter into controversy with the external other. This, in turn, invites clarification but often leads to confusion and quibbling. Thus we have not yet established the critical limits of our explanatory power. But in the relation of contrariety, the concepts are governed by another that differs in kind and that admits of no contingency. Here the likeness and difference are tied to each other, and the relationship is specific. From this view the concepts are diametrically opposed yet equally bound together. Such a formulation shows the mutual dependence of terms; they are such-and-such relation and cannot be otherwise. A brief list of these common antinomies includes materialism and idealism; individual and society; freedom and necessity; pleasure and pain; *Gemeinschaft* and *Gesellschaft*; coercion and consensus; public and private; theory and praxis; work and leisure; trust and distrust. Hence in the sphere of contrariety the terms present themselves as immediately unlike yet implying their opposites. They are not related in mere outline or rough approximation; rather they are enclosed and strictly accounted for.

It is important to notice that this orientation to knowledge of the bifurcated nature of the political world, at once self-dependent yet linked, can go awry easily. The danger arises in holding that all conditions that we are seeking to elucidate are or can be opposed. Whether we can use the corelatedness level of explanation depends upon the medium or nature of political reality. Clearly *consensus* and *pain* bear no relation to each other. Thus at this level of analysis, all political notions may be considered distinct but not necessarily corelated.

To this same point can be added that although the determination of corelations is of the most compelling interest inasmuch as rigor and accuracy are sought, these three methods of investigation are not divorced by any means. Identification, differentiation, and mediation are not at odds with each other. Each mode of analysis in its particular way enhances the intelligibility of the terms. From the former two directions alone spring distinction, difference, and classification. The third consideration, contrariety, deserves the greatest emphasis, for this approach revitalizes and preserves the one-sided aspects of identity and difference. It is a larger-scale analysis that contains the earlier components and yet also gives rise to a necessarily new dimension of explanation: identity in difference.

The attraction, if not the significant power, of this qualitative account of political conceptions rests on the recognition that the sphere of political knowledge is limited, and its intelligibility inevitably depends on its consistent defense of its own borders. In trying to redress balances, the method of analysis I have suggested approaches the subject in a dynamic, sequential manner. It provides an analytical framework by which the many-dimensioned concepts and relations come to the fore and can be appreciated fully.

For a long time the attention of political researches has been distracted from qualitative, categorical thinking, instead attending to mathematical models, probabilistic approaches, and directly measurable political attitudes. This development was certainly not a product of a few years or decades. Quantification, in the sense used here, began to acquire a definite meaning in the early part of the seventeenth century. Its application to political thought occurred chiefly because modern thought allowed itself to become more and more animated by the demonstrable truths and precision of the exact sciences. It would be folly to believe that the tenor of future political inquiries will steer away from quantitative standpoints. One can, however, guard against determinations according to multitude, which, especially in our own time, have clouded determinations according to kind.

Notes

1. John W. Burgess, *Political Science and Comparative Constitutional Law* (Boston, 1896), vol. 1, p. vi. See also Bernard E. Brown, *American Conservatives: The Political Thought of Francis Lieber and John W. Burgess* (New York, 1951), and Albert Somit and Joseph Tanenhaus, *The Development of Political Science* (Boston, 1967), chap. 2.

2. William B. Munro, *The Invisible Government* (New York, 1928), p. 33.

3. Albert Shaw, "Presidential Address," *American Political Science Review* 1 (February 1907): 181.

4. Jesse Macy, "The Scientific Spirit in Politics," *American Political Science Review* 2 (February 1917): 6–7.

5. Charles E. Merriam, *New Aspects of Politics* (Chicago, 1925), p. xxx.

6. G. E. G. Catlin, *The Science and Method of Politics* (London, 1927), p. 112.

7. Floyd H. Allport, "Political Science and Psychology," in *The Social Sciences and their Interrelations*, ed. William Ogburn (Boston, 1927), p. 277.

8. See Richard Fagen, "Some Contributions of Mathematical Reasoning to the Study of Politics," *American Political Science Review* 55 (December 1976): 888–99.

9. See Floyd H. Allport, "A Technique for the Measurement and Analysis of Public Opinion," *Proceedings of the American Sociological Society* 20 (1926): 241–44. See also polls by the American Institute of Public Opinion and the National Opinion Research Center.

10. See, for example, Butler's satire in *Hudibras*, ed. John Wilders (Oxford, 1967), 1.i.119–26:

In *Mathematicka* he was greater
Then *Tycho Brahe* or *Erra Pater*:
For he by *Geometrick* scale
Could take the size of *Pots* of Ale;
Resolve by Sines and Tangents straight,
If *Bread* or *Butter* wanted weight;
And wisely tell what hour o' th'
The Clock does strike, by *Algebra*

See also Johann Eckermann, *Conversations with Goethe* (London, 1970), p. 139; Samuel Coleridge, *Poems* (London, 1974), p. 8. In the discipline of history, R. G. Collingwood, in his *Idea of History* (Oxford, 1946), has provided a major, high-quality account and critique of this trend. Only recently has sociology attempted to divest itself of positivistic programs. See David Frisby, ed., *The Positivist Dispute in German Sociology* (London, 1976).

11. These discussions can be found in the following: William Elliot, *The Pragmatic Revolt in Politics* (New York, 1928); Edward Corwin, "The Democratic Dogma and the Future of Political Science," *American Political Science Review* 23 (August 1929): 569–92; J. Mark Jacobsen, "Evaluating State Administrative Structure—The Fallacy of the Statistical Approach," *American Political Science Review* 22 (November 1928): 928–35; Helmut Schoeck and James Wiggins, eds., *Scientism and Values* (Princeton, 1960); James Charlesworth, *The Limits of Behavioralism in Political Science: A Symposium* (Philadelphia, 1962); Eric Weil, "Philosophie politique, théorie politique," *Revue française de science politique* 11 (June 1961); Bernard Crick, *The American Science of Politics* (London, 1959), chaps. 11, 12.

12. Hegel, *Philosophy of Right*, trans. T. M. Knox (Oxford, 1942), sec. 1.

13. Jeremy Bentham, *An Introduction to the Principles of Morals and Legislation* (London, 1823), xvii, sec. 25 note.

14. See Aristotle, *Categories*, in *The Works of Aristotle*, ed. W. D. Ross (Oxford, 1928), 10a27.

15. Consider, for example, the formula advanced by Karl Deutsch to explain the political notion of stability ($St = (G/L\ pol) \times (y/y10)$) where: g indicates the percentage of government spending within the national budget, L the percentage of literacy, *pol* the extent of political participation, y the percentage of per-capita national income, $y10$ the highest 10 percent income recipients. "Toward an Inventory of Basic Trends and Patterns in Comparative and International Politics," *American Political Science Review* 54 (March 1960): 36. This is illustrative of "cookbook" attempts to give qualitative postulates quantitative forms.

16. Aristotle, *Categories*, 11a15.

17. In Hobbes, for example, both authority and power are viewed as distinct from one another. See Hobbes, *English Works*, ed. W. Molesworth (London, 1839), vol. 3, pp. 85–86, vol. 4. pp. 37–38. In another sense, however, Hobbes spoke of power and authority as connected to one another in that authority ("sovereign" authority) presupposed the legitimate exercise of power. See ibid., vol. 3, pp. 163–64, 199. Robert Dahl, to provide another illustration, uses the terms *power, influence, control,* and *authority* interchangeably. See his "Concept of Power," *Behavioral Science* 3 (July 1957): 202.

18. See Stanley Rothman, *European Society and Politics* (New York, 1970), pp. 38ff.

Bibliography

Adam, C. *La Philosophie de Francois Bacon*. Paris, 1890.

Alker, R. "Measuring Inequality," *The Quantitative Analysis of Social Problems*. Edited by E. R. Tufte. Reading, Mass.: Addison-Wesley, 1970.

Anderson, F. H. *The Philosophy of Francis Bacon*. New York: Octagon Books, 1971.

———. *Francis Bacon, His Career and His Thought*. Los Angeles, Calif., 1962.

Armstrong, R. L. *Metaphysics and British Empiricism*. Lincoln, Neb.: University of Nebraska Press, 1970.

Aubrey, J. *Letters and Lives of Eminent Men*. London, 1813.

Avenant, 'd', C. *Political and Commercial Works*. 5 vols. London, 1771.

Bacon, Francis.

    Essays. Edited by F. Storr and C. H. Gibson. Third ed. London: Longmans, Green & Co., 1891.

    Novum Organum. Edited by Thomas Fowler. Oxford, 1878.

    The Letters and Life of Francis Bacon. Edited by J. Spedding. London, 1861.

    Works. Edited by J. M. Robertson. London and New York, 1905.

    Works. Edited by J. Spedding, R. L. Ellis, and D. D. Heath. London: Longman & Co., 1857–1874.

Bain, A. *John Stuart Mill: A Criticism*. London: Longman & Co., 1882.

Bayles, M. D. "Mill's Utilitarianism and Aristotle's Rhetoric," *The Modern Schoolman* 51 (January 1974).

Benson, O. "The Mathematical Approach to Political Science," *Contempo-

rary Political Analysis. Edited by J. Charlesworth. New York: Free Press, 1967.

Bernd, J. L. (ed.) *Mathematical Application in Political Science*. Charlottesville, Va.: University of Virginia Press, 1964.

Birch, T. *The History of the Royal Society for Improving of Natural Knowledge*. 4 vols. London, Royal Society, 1756.

Black, M. *The Nature of Mathematics*. New York: Kegan Paul, 1933.

Blake, R. M., Ducasse, C. J., and Madden, E. H. *Theories of Scientific Method: The Renaissance through the Nineteenth Century*. Seattle: University of Washington Press, 1960.

Blunt, H. W. "Bacon's Method of Science," *Proceedings of the Aristotelian Society* 4 (1903–1904).

Bowle, J. *Hobbes and His Critics*. London: Cape, 1951.

Brandt, F. *Thomas Hobbes' Mechanical Conception of Nature*. Copenhagen: Levin & Munksguard, 1928.

Broad, C. D. *The Philosophy of Bacon*. Cambridge: Cambridge University Press, 1926.

Brown, K. C. (ed). *Hobbes' Studies*. Oxford: Blackwell, 1965.

Buchanan, J. M., Tullock, G. *The Calculus of Consent*. Ann Arbor: University of Michigan Press, 1962.

Burtt, E. A. *The Metaphysical Foundations of Modern Physical Science*. London: Kegan Paul, 1925.

Catlin, G. *Thomas Hobbes as Philosopher, Publicist and Man of Letters*. Oxford: Blackwell, 1922.

Church, R. W. *Bacon*. London: Macmillan, 1884.

Churchman, C. W., Ratoosh, P. (eds). *Measurement: Definitions and Theories*. New York: Wiley, 1959.

Comte, A. *Cours de Philosophie Positive*. 6 vols. Paris, 1830–42.

Crapulli, G. *Mathesis Universalis*. Rome, 1969.

Davey, N. (ed). *British Scientific Literature in the Seventeenth Century*. London, 1953.

Davidson, W. L. *Political Thought in England*. Westport, Conn.: Hyperion Press, 1979.

Devey, J. *The Physical and Metaphysical Works of Lord Bacon*. London, 1853.

Dickie, W. M. "A Comparison of the Scientific Method and Achievement of Aristotle and Bacon," *Philosophical Review* 31 (1922).

Ducasse, C. J. "Francis Bacon's Philosophy of Science," *Theories of Scientific Method: The Renaissance Through the Nineteenth Century*, R. M. Blake, C. J. Ducasse, and E. H. Madden. Seattle, 1960.

Edgeworth, F. *Mathematical Psychics: An Essay on the Application of Mathematics to the Moral Sciences*. London: Kegan Paul, 1881.

Farrington, B. *Francis Bacon: Philosopher of Industrial Science*. London: Lawrence & Wishart, 1951.

Feuerbach, L. *Geschichte der Neueren Philosophie von Bacon bis Spinoza*. Stuttgart, 1906.

Fischer, K. *Francis Bacon of Verulum: Realistic Philosophy and Its Age*. Trans. by John Oxenford. London, 1857.

Florian, P. "De Bacon à Newton," *Revue de Philosophie* 24 (1914).

Fontenelle, B. "Preface to the Memoirs of the Royal Academy at Paris, in the Year 1699, treating of the Usefulness of Mathematical Learning," *Miscellanea Curiso* of the Royal Society. London, 1726.

Fulton, J. F. "The Rise of Experimental Method: Bacon and the Royal Society of London," *Yale Journal of Biology and Medicine* (March 1931).

Gauthier, D. P. *The Logic of Leviathan*. Oxford: Clarendon Press, 1969.

Gilbert, N. W. *Renaissance Concepts of Method*. New York: Columbia University Press, 1960.

Goldsmith, M. M. *Hobbes' Science of Politics*. New York: Columbia University Press, 1966.

Granger, G. *La mathématique sociale du marquis de Condorcet*. Paris, 1956.

Graunt, J. *Natural and Political Observations on the Bills of Mortality*. London, 1676.

Guénon, R. *Le règne de la quantité et les signes des temps*. Paris, Gallimard, 1945.

Gurr, T. *Politimetrics. An Introduction to Quantitative Macropolitics*. Englewood Cliffs, N.J.: Prentice-Hall, 1972.

Hacker, A. "The Utility of Quantitative Methods in Political Science," *Contemporary Political Analysis*. Edited by J. Charlesworth. New York: Free Press, 1967.

Hall, M. B. *The Scientific Renaissance, 1450–1630*. London: Fontana, 1970.

Harvey, H. "Hobbes and Descartes in the Light of some Unpublished Letters," *Osiris* 10 (1962).

Heath, I. L. *A History of Greek Mathematics*. 2 vols. Oxford, 1921.

Heiberg, J. L. *Mathematics and Physical Science in Classical Antiquity*. Trans. by D. C. Macgregor. London: Oxford University Press, 1922.

Heidel, W. "Qualitative Change in Pre-Socratic Philosophy," *Achiv zur Geschichte der Philosophie* 19 (1906).

Hobbes, Thomas.
    Cogitate Physico-Mathematica, 1644.
    Decameron Physiologicum, or Ten Dialogues of Natural Philosophy, 1678.

De Cive or The Citizen. Edited by S. P. Lamprecht, New York, 1949.

De Corpore Politico, or The Elements of Law, Moral and Politics, 1650.

De Principiis et Rationcinatione Geometrarum, 1666.

English Works. Edited by W. Molesworth. 11 vols. London, 1839–1845.

Leviathan. Edited by M. Oakeshott. Oxford, 1946; J. Plamenatz, 1962.

Lux Mathematica, 1672.

Principia et Problemata, 1672.

The Questions concerning Liberty, Necessity, and Chance, 1656.

Rosetum Geometricum, 1671.

Seven Philosophical Problems and Two Propositions of Geometry, 1682.

T. Hobbes Malmesburiensis Vita, 1679.

Tractatus Opticus, 1644.

Hochberg, H. "The Empirical Philosophy of Roger and Francis Bacon," *Philosophy of Science* 20 (1953).

Jessop, T. E. *Thomas Hobbes.* London: Longmans, 1960.

Jones, R. F. "Science and Language in England in the mid-Seventeenth Century," *The Seventeenth Century.* Stanford, Calif.: Stanford University Press, 1951.

King, G. *Natural and Political Observations and Conclusions on State and Condition of England,* 1696.

Klein, J. *Greek Mathematical Thought and the Origin of Algebra.* Trans. by E. Brann. Cambridge, Mass.: M.I.T. Press, 1968.

Knights, L. C. "Bacon and the Dissociation of Sensibility," *Explorations* (1946).

Koyré, A. *Metaphysics and Measurements: Essays in Scientific Revolution.* Cambridge: Harvard University Press, 1968.

———. "The Origins of Modern Science," *Diogenes* 16 (Winter 1956).

Krajewski, W. "The Law of the Connection of Quality to Quantity," *Dialectics and Humanism* 1 (Winter 1974).

Lalande, A. *Quid de Mathematica Senserit Baconus Verulamus,* 1899.

Lasswell, H. D. et al. *Language of Politics: Studies in Quantitative Semantics.* New York: G. W. Stewart, 1949.

———, Lasswell, H. D. (ed). "Qualitative Measurement in the Social Sciences: Classification, Typologies and Indices," *The Policy Sciences.* Stanford, Calif., Stanford University Press, 1951.

Lazarfeld, P. F. *Mathematical Thinking in the Social Sciences.* Glencoe, Illinois: Free Press, 1954.

Lemmi, C. W. *The Classical Deities in Bacon.* Baltimore: Johns Hopkins Press, 1933.

Lerner, D. (ed). *Quantity and Quality* (The Hayden Colloquium on Scientific Method and Concept, MIT). New York: Free Press of Glencoe, 1961.

Letwin, S. *On the Pursuit of Certainty.* Cambridge: Cambridge University Press, 1965

Lévy-Bruhl, L. *Introduction, Letters Inédites de John Stuart Mill à Auguste Comte.* Paris, 1899.

Macaulay, T. B. "Mill's Essay on Government," *Edinburgh Review* 49 (March 1829).

Macdonald, H. and Hargreaves, M. *Thomas Hobbes, A Bibliography.* London: The Bibliographical Society, 1952.

Macpherson, C. B. *The Political Theory of Possessive Individualism.* Oxford: Clarendon Press, 1962.

Marsak, L. M. (ed). *The Rise of Science in Relation to Society.* New York: Macmillan, 1964.

McClure, M. T. "Francis Bacon and the Modern Spirit," *Journal of Philosophy* 14 (1917).

McNeilly, F. S. *The Anatomy of Leviathan.* London: Macmillan, 1968.

Merton, R. K. *Science, Technology and Society in Seventeenth Century England.* Atlantic Highlands, N.J.: Humanities Press, 1970.

Mill, John Stewart.

A System of Logic. 2 vols. London, 1843.

Auguste Comte and Positivism. Reprinted from the *Westminster Review,* 83 (April 1865), 84 (July 1865). London, 1907.

Autobiography. Edited by Helen Taylor. London, 1873.

Considerations on Representative Government. London, 1861.

On Liberty. London, 1859.

Principles of Political Economy. 2 vols. London, 1848.

The Subjection of Women. London, 1869.

Utilitarianism. London, 1863.

Mintz, S. I. *The Hunting of Leviathan.* Cambridge: University Press, 1962.

Montricla, J. F. *Histoire des Mathématiques.* 2nd ed. 4 vols. Paris, 1799–1802, reprinted 1960.

Moritz, A. "Notes and Documents—Thomas Hobbes and Samuel Sorbriere," *Revue Germanique* (April 1908).

Mueller, I. W. *John Stuart Mill and French Thought.* Urbana: University of Illinois Press, 1956.

Nagel, E. *On the Logic of Measurement.* A Thesis. New York, 1930.

Nagel, E. *John Stuart Mill's Philosophy of Scientific Method.* New York: Hafner Publishing Co., 1950.

Napier, M. *Remarks Illustrative of the Scope and Influence of the Philosophical Writings of Lord Bacon.* Edinburgh, 1818.

Nichol, J. *Francis Bacon, the Life and Philosophy*. Edinburgh, 1889.

Ornstein, M. *The Role of Scientific Societies in the Seventeenth Century*. Chicago: University of Chicago Press, 1928.

Packe, M. *The Life of John Stuart Mill*. London: Secker & Warburg, 1954.

Parel, A. (ed). *The Political Calculus: Essays on Machiavelli's Philosophy*. Toronto: University of Toronto Press, 1972.

Penrose, S. B. "The Reputation and Influence of Francis Bacon in the Seventeenth Century." PhD dissertation. New York, 1934.

Peters, R. *Hobbes*. Harmondsworth: Penguin Books, 1956.

Petty, W. *Political Arithmetick*. London, 1690.

Plamenatz, J. P. *The English Utilitarians*. Oxford: Blackwell, 1958.

Primack, M. "Outline of a Reinterpretation of Francis Bacon's Philosophy," *Journal of the History of Philosophy* 5 (1967).

Prior, M. E. "Bacon's Man of Science," *Journal of the History of Ideas* 15 (1954).

Randall, J. "J. S. Mill's Empiricism," *Journal of the History of Ideas* 26 (January–March 1965).

Rashevsky, N. *Mathematical Biology of Social Behavior*. Chicago: University of Chicago Press, 1951.

Reichenbach, H. *The Rise of Scientific Philosophy*. Berkeley, Calif.: University of California Press, 1951.

Reid, T. "An Essay on Quantity," *Essays on the Powers of the Human Mind*, vol. 1. Edinburgh, 1819.

Rigault, M. H. *Histoire de la Querelle: Des Anciens et des Modernes*. Paris, 1856.

Riker, W., Ordeshook, P. *An Introduction to Positive Political Theory*. Englewood Cliffs, N.J.: Prentice-Hall, 1973.

Robson, J. M. *The Improvement of Mankind: The Social and Political Thought of John Stuart Mill*. London: Routledge & Kegan Paul, 1968.

Rossi, P. *Francis Bacon: From Magic to Science*. Trans. by S. Rabinovitch. Chicago: University of Chicago Press, 1968.

Royal Society. "Quantities, Units, and Symbols," *A Report by the Symbols Committee*, 2nd ed. (6 March 1975).

Sambursky, S. *The Physical World of the Greeks*. Trans. by Merton Dagut. London: Routledge & Kegan Paul, 1963.

Sartori, G., Riggs, F., Teune, H. *Tower of Babel: On the Definition and Analysis of Concepts in the Social Sciences* 6 (1975).

Schaub, E. L. "Francis Bacon and the Modern Spirit," *Monist* 40 (1930).

Sortais, G. *La Philosophie moderne, depuis Bacon jusqu'à Leibniz*. Paris, 1920.

Spragens, T. A. *The Politics of Motion*. London: Croom Helm, 1973.

Sprat, T. *The History of the Royal Society of London, for the Improving of Natural Knowledge*. London, 1667.

Stephen, L. *Hobbes*. London: Macmillan, 1904.

————. *The English Utilitarians*. 3 vols. London: Duckworth, 1900.

Strauss, L. *The Political Philosophy of Hobbes, Its Basis and Genesis*. Oxford: Clarendon Press, 1936.

Strong, E. W. *Procedures and Metaphysics: a study in the philosophy of mathematical-physical science in the sixteenth and seventeenth centuries*. Berkeley: University of California Press, 1936.

Taine, H. *English Positivism, A Study of J. S. Mill*, 1870.

Taylor, A. E. "Francis Bacon," *Proceedings of the British Academy* 12 (1926).

Tulluck, G. *Toward a Mathematics of Politics*. Ann Arbor: University of Michigan Press 1967.

Vaysset-Boutbien, R. *Stuart Mill et la sociologie francaise contemporaine*. Paris, 1941.

Vialatoux, J. *La Cité de Hobbes: Theorie de l'Etat totalitaire*. Paris, 1935.

Warrender, J. H. *The Political Philosophy of Hobbes*. Oxford:. Clarendon Press, 1957.

Watkins, J. W. N. *Hobbes's System of Ideas*. London: Hutchinson University Library, 1965.

Weber, M. *Economy and Society*. 3 vols. Edited by G. Roth and C. Wittich. New York: Bedminster Press, 1968.

Wetter, G. A. "The Law of the Transition from Quantity to Quality," *Dialectical Materialism*. London, 1958.

Whewell, W. *Of Induction*. London, 1849.

White, B. *Peace Among the Willows*. The Hague: Martinez Nijhoff, 1968.

Wilkins, J. *Mathematical Magick: or the wonders that may be performed by mechanical geometry*. London, 1648.

Willey, B. *The Seventeenth Century Background*. London: Chatto & Windus, 1934.

————. *The English Moralists*. New York: Norton, 1965.

Wolin, S. S. *Hobbes and the Epic Tradition of Political Theory*. Los Angeles: University of California Press, 1970.

Woolf, Harry (ed). *Quantification: A History of the Meaning of Measurement in the Natural and Social Sciences*. New York: Bobbs-Merrill, 1961.

Yule, G. "The Introduction of the Words 'Statistics,' 'Statistical,' into the English Language," *Journal of the Royal Statistical Society* 68 (1905).

Zamyatin, Y. *We*. Harmondsworth: Penguin Books, 1970.
Zilsel, E. "The Sociological Roots of Science," *The American Journal of Sociology* 47 (1941–1942).

Index

About the Author

ROBERT SCHWARE is a political scientist at the National Center for Atmospheric Research, Advanced Study Program, Boulder, Colorado. Previously he.was with the Aspen Institute for Humanistic Studies. He holds a Ph.D. degree in government from the London School of Economics and Political Science.